I am come into my garden, my sister, my bride;
I have gathered my myrrh with my spice;
I have eaten my honeycomb with my honey;
I have drunk my wine with my milk.
Eat, O friends;
Drink, yea,
drink abundantly,
O beloved!

The Bible: The Song of Songs

$\mathcal{I}$ AM COME
INTO MY GARDEN

I AM COME INTO MY GARDEN

ALLAN WARGON

A Love Story

A Patrick Crean Book

SOMERVILLE HOUSE PUBLISHING
TORONTO

Canadian Cataloguing in Publication Data

Wargon, Allan
I am come into my garden : a love story
Poem.

ISBN 1-895897-20-3

1. Title.

PS8595.A7412   1995   c811'.54   C95-930735-4
PR9199.3.W3712   1995

Design: Gordon Robertson
Cover photograph: Barbara Cole
Author photograph: Harold Whyte

Biblical verse reprinted by courtesy of The Jewish
Publication Society of America, from the Holy Scriptures
according to the Masoretic text, 1917 edition.

Printed in Canada

A Patrick Crean Book

Published by Somerville House Publishing,
a division of Somerville House Books Limited:
3080 Yonge Street, Suite 5000, Toronto, Ontario M4N 3N1

Somerville House Publishing acknowledges the financial assistance of
the Ontario Publishing Centre, the Ontario Arts Council, the Ontario
Development Corporation and the Department of Communications.

1

A YEAR
ALONE

There's a path from the far side of the bridge
to the little cabin where I write
that for the past week I've had to walk with care
because of the violets that have appeared in it.
The woods are gently carpeted with them now,
mauve and yellow and white, their delicate heads
set off by the pretty, frilled, usually heart-shaped leaves.
If on a desert island I could have only two flowers
my second choice would be the violet,
to remind me of all that is graceful, simple, and pure.
My first choice would be the rose; for the rose —
like the Bible — is everything.

Although I've made the farm a wildlife sanctuary,
within its boundaries the natural cycle of life,
unsparing of the weak and unwary, goes on undisturbed.

At noon today the dogs caught a groundhog behind the house;
and then one of the barn cats, not yet fully grown,
and with a face so innocent you'd think its owner incapable
of hurting even a mouse, brought into the stable a partridge,
a bird almost as big as itself, and one that is prized by gourmets.
Later that afternoon I found a morel, a mushroom that is to this terrain
what the truffle is to France.

So we all ate well.

Along with my morel, which I browned lightly in butter
and served myself as a small separate dish,
I had my daily salad of dandelion leaves;
they are smooth and tasty at this time of year.

There's an abundance of edible wild plants within yards of this house,
but I don't have time to gather and prepare them;
so I confine myself to the greens that grow outside the kitchen door,
and they fill in nicely until the first lettuce comes from the garden.

Each spring there's a new crop of stones.
Pushed up by frost from the rocky subsoil, then tiller mixed
with the fine dark loam, they are velvety stones;
they caress my hands as I lob them into the garden lane,
where over the years I've built up a hard-packed, almost-level road.
That's a rare thing in this narrow V-shaped valley,

4

with its steep, tree-covered slopes, which open only to the south —
to the sun, and sometimes to a warm wind
when one manages to ride in on the swift, north-flowing stream.
All other winds are solidly shut out; in winter, storms rage overhead
while down below, where the buildings are, it's often sunny and still.

The buildings are clustered beside or near the water;
the fields roll out above, on the high plateau through which the river,
probably preceded by a glacier, once cut, and still cuts, its way.
Around the fields the dense hardwood forest is filled with woodland life,
and the spring-fed rollicking river is clean and full of fish.

In this blessed realm I'm a solitary servant;
I pay the taxes and mend the wear and tear.

It's good being alone with my thoughts; it's what I wanted.
But my empty bed, the silent house, the lack of female smells
leave a dull yearning. Before coming here
I knew at the same time three beautiful women,
and each charged and charmed the air, and made eating a divine delight;
but I grew weary of their sighs and silent reproaches,
of dark envy underlying even the ecstatic hours,
of being burdened by my own tenacious guilt.

I had been much with people,
they had crowded my days and occupied my nights;

my spirit craved a rest. The years here have been refreshing,
but a shared life seems behind me now.
I seldom meet women anymore, and those I'm drawn to
are always already married. Besides, though I need beauty and charm
I'd like as well someone who understands my roots,
and who can excite my soul.

   She's very often in my dreams,
that imagined companion I might never know.
Without her I doubt that I would bare these thoughts,
or bother phrasing the reports of eyes and nose and ears.
And though it's a kind of folly, and absurd,
some conscious self-delusion helps to keep me balanced here.
Taste, for instance of food, is enhanced if I make believe it's shared,
and the touch of anything I can fantasize as being of skin.
And when there's beauty so acute it hurts,
or fleeting magic, or tenderness that wants to overflow,
then I need her most, and instantly she's there,
formless and faceless, of course, but with, I feel,
a shrewd understanding in her look, and, it follows,
the warning of a mocking smile around her mouth.

Behind the house, alongside the river, ending at a dam
that forms a swimming pool some ten feet deep with rock bottom and sides,
there's a second garden that retains a hint of formality,
though it's been neglected for the past two or three years.
The dam, which was opened for repair and the adding
     of an automatic gate,
was never closed because I ran out of money and didn't buy the thing,
and since then the river has flowed at its natural level.
The flower beds have lost their definition and become
     crowded with weeds,
the borders are ragged, and under some of the trees
there lies a carpet of last autumn's leaves.
    I laid out this garden in a burst of baronial pride,
which soon faded, and from that time on I've done little in it,
except to prune a few trees that produce particularly tangy apples.
    This afternoon I went back there to get a clump of peony
for a sunny space beside the front door of the house,
and found, in the center of the main bed,
a cluster of lovely tulips I had forgotten about.
They were erect and fresh from the shower this morning,
their svelte heads spangled with rain drops,
and their petals — white, edged with shocking pink —
were demurely, almost provocatively, closed.
    When I was digging the peonies I suddenly saw a morel.

It was in the grass only a few feet away. Then I saw another,
and another, and two more — six, eight, eleven, fifteen —
the grass under the apple trees was dotted with morels!
Three weeks ago I had been elated to find a single one,
and all the time there had been a glut of them,
only twenty yards from the kitchen door.
    I picked two handfuls, but alas, they were all over-ripe.
Another person, less busy than I, would surely have seen them.

    Even in daylight I now think of her,
noticing her by the water or among the trees,
or going uphill, or walking freely in the fields.
Sometimes she watches while I work, and talks with me,
and once I was quite startled by her as I shaved,
and cut myself, and both of us, after our surprise, laughed heartily.
She charms me; whether she's blonde or brown, black, auburn or gray,
I'm moved by her: for moments she almost lifts me from myself.
Almost. Because I know it's need that sees her through my eyes,
and loneliness that gives her such vivacity and wit,
and despair, at least a bit, that keeps me from presuming her love.
But never mind, I sublimate by using my surroundings,
which brings other pleasures — discovery, insight, amusement,
and often, encouragingly, even joy.

Such feathered splendor this spring —
I don't remember ever seeing so many birds,
or in such profusion of color.

Creamy birds that look as if they'd just bathed in milk,
and others that are pale lemon-yellow shading to butterscotch;
and then those streaks of sunshine, the bright goldfinches,
or *wild canaries* as most people call them.
Birds the soft color of unpainted Florida oranges;
others the pale copper of autumn leaves framed by wings
      like brown earth,
and of course the comfortable red-brown breasts of robins.

And scarlet. Yesterday a tanager sat in full sunlight
on a willow branch over the pond; I set down what I was carrying,
ordered the dogs to stay put, and moved closer for a better look —
but the bird noticed and flew off to hide among the cedars
on the other bank. Then there are rose-breasted grosbeaks,
and the garish red crest on the head of the idiot woodpecker
who attacks the metal downspouts on the barn,
surely knowing by now that such trees yield no grubs,
but enjoying the resounding tat-tat-tat-tat his bill makes.

Some mornings when I go out there are mallards on the pond,
wearing their collars of iridescent green,
and any day now — though I haven't seen one yet this year —
a moving blur will hover for an instant and I'll have a glimpse

of the shimmering, evanescent green of the hummingbird.
   And there are plenty of bluish birds:
jays and kingfishers are always darting around the house,
a heron occasionally visits the pond,
and once in a while — though rarely — I see the shy bluebird,
which is a color like the clearest blue of sky and water mixed.
Then there are the gorgeous glossy black birds
who carry themselves with an aristocratic air,
none of which I know by name.
   I see I've missed the swallows nesting under the bridge,
the friendly chickadees, the raucous crows and many more —
but, a lot of birds, and I'm glad to have them.

   One result of being alone
is that it takes me out of time:
what was, and is, and might yet be
all run together; life becomes
this inner continuity
of key emotional moments,
and only they come to matter.

Lark-*ie* was a laughing girl
to whose family name we kids soon added
that singing suffix, because she so often seemed to soar
high above the rest of us. A gilded girl,
with golden freckles and sunny hair, and a smile so bright
it lit the day, and lit in me, from then on,
like an inner flame, an image of my joy in women.
I was crazy mad for her, but secretly;
with the difference in our ages — she was eight, I twelve,
it was not to be thought of.

Today I changed the storm windows for screens
— late as usual — and the house is filled with moving breezes,
soft rustlings, and the sound of rushing water.
Starting when the first shoots of crocus emerge from the snow,
the atmosphere inside, pent up from long months of enclosure,
seems to thicken impatiently until it bursts forth
when the slabs of glass are removed,
and then a rush of fragrant air sweeps through,
scattering papers and unsettling the staid routines of winter.

But I recall that in November,
when the storm windows go on again,
there is relief in the softening of sound
and a pleasant expectation of the deepening quiet of snow.

It's when I've tidied up and changed the bed,
folding the fresh sheet back across the blanket,
and there are flowers in the room, a book, a candle,
that I miss a woman most. No wishful thinking then,
but only a deep wanting for the female forms,
for the different, undiscovered, maybe unforced mind,
for the way the erotically-empty atmosphere
becomes suddenly and excitingly filled.

A fat garter snake has taken up residence in the garden.
Whatever its sex, I call her Bertha, because she has the girth
to go with that round-sounding name. She's perfectly harmless —
except to insects, and possibly to small frogs and mice —
which makes her a sort of self-appointed guardian of plants

that are otherwise protected only by their own good health,
because I don't use chemical fertilizers, herbicides or pesticides
        of any kind.
    Sometimes I notice Bertha gliding purposefully
through the grass along the border as if she knows
where there's a good morsel at that moment, but most often
I disturb her when she's lazily curled among the strawberries,
or under the rhubarb leaves. She is quite secure in the garden;
for none of her natural enemies will venture close with the dogs around,
while they seem to regard her as an alien being,
and observe her movements with half shut, uninterested eyes.

    We speak of the first day of summer,
but already, before that day begins,
the night of the longest day has passed and summer has begun to wane.
How quickly the surge of growth passes in this northern land!
In March, still under the snows of winter,
it begins to feel the warmth of the returning sun;
in April it is stirring, thrusting up first shoots
through the moist cover of last year's leaves;
in May it is irrepressible —
neither lingering patches of snow nor late frosts can blunt
        its steady unfolding,

and in June it bursts forth in a riotous tropical rush.

    Then it is over.

Even in the heat of July grasses grow less quickly,

some leaves — scarcely opened, it seems — start to yellow,

        plants go to seed.

The nights of August are turning cool

before the ripened grain is brought in from the fields.

September retains its splendid fullness,

but one feels it is the last, that nothing fresh and green will follow.

Then the golden cascades of October glow briefly

in the rays of the retreating sun;

and November comes on cool and frowning,

spreading ice on puddles that grayly reflect clouds heavy with snow.

Jerry, the physics teacher who's to spend the summer here,

arrived as expected along with his *almost fourteen*-year-old daughter Nicki

and her friend Amelia. I offered them the empty other house,

but they chose to stay with me; the girls are to help with the cooking,

and to serve. They're a delightful pair;

they emerge from the adolescent messiness of their room —

It's okay: we've hidden our unmentionables at the bottom of our suitcases!

— to pick charming bouquets of wild flowers,

and they conspire for long murmuring periods, broken by fits of giggling,

in the dining room and the purposely-darkened kitchen.
At mealtimes, flushed with success, they flounce out with their offerings
— some hot, some cold because *You guys are so darn late!* —
and then wryly run back for missing napkins, knives and forks.
We dine with relish and great good humor.

We've begun haying. Not having any of the do-everything machines,
we cut and crimp and bale, draw the bales in and stack them
in separate operations. We've been taking in our neighbor's hay,
then he and his family will help with ours;
it is a bustling, friendly, happy time.
The sun spreads its molten heat over shining fields,
swarms of little orange butterflies suck honeyed nectar
          from milkweed blooms,
and the warm air is heavy with a hundred scents
as wild flowers and shrubs exude their fragrant oils;
while round us the sweet odor of fresh sweat
mingles with the heady perfume of the new hay.

The last thing we do on the last evening of haying
is to carry the long bale elevator back from the driving shed to the barn.
The same four had carried it out earlier in the day,
but we were fresher then: weights tend to get heavier
after we've heaved hundreds of bales. As the proprietor
I again take the heaviest corner, the one with the motor,
and as we go along I sense that this time it's too heavy
for my tired muscles to support. But I say nothing; it's only later,
when we get up from a needed snack, that pain tells me
the *strongest-boy-in-the-world* has strained a stomach muscle.
Now, I have several times moved that elevator by myself,
but never by trying to carry it; always I devised some roller or lever
that supported its main weight. I could have done the same
for that last moving of it; but a spirit of bravado enters into men
when they act together, the same spirit that sends them perilously
into play and war.

Nicki and Amelia are magnetic;
my eyes go to them whenever I think they might not see,
but they always do, and then their movements and their merriment

take on a subtle, added element of show. Those imps know
they're tempting: they strut about in their skimpy shorts and blouses,
seductively swaying their fresh little breasts and bottoms,
and trying not to smirk; they feel, instinctively, that here
it's a safe game, that Jerry and I will only look
and maybe, in fantasy, long; but *oh no!* — should it
even for a flicker turn real, those shocked, frightened nymphs
would silently, swiftly and righteously point out
that we, poor fools, are merely the pawns they practice on.

This afternoon I go up to disk the field
that was to have been sown in buckwheat, but which,
      not being ready in time,
will now be kept in summer fallow. Between it and the pasture field
I had left a hedgerow some ten feet wide, intended as a nesting place
      for birds,
those traditional guardians of crops on whom farmers turned their backs
when they began spraying with poisonous insecticides.
Last year a line of white spruce was planted in the hedgerow,
and this spring, to fill it out as a windbreak,
I added three-hundred Carolina poplar, spacing them at even intervals
about a pace inside the permanent fence.
    So it is with intense dismay

that I see that the cattle have broken through the temporary fence
on the pasture side of the hedgerow
and, following their custom,
have marched in file along the other fence —
right on the row of poplar. Three hundred trees!
Now only a few splintered stalks remain.
    But when I come down for supper
        and pause to look at the flower beds
Jerry has been weeding I see in one — a dry flinty bed
        beside the garage —
a cluster of strange plants, and suddenly remember
that it was there I had tossed a few shriveled seed pods
        of a flaming poppy
I had picked four years ago in a friend's garden in Quebec
and had found this spring, crumpled and dusty,
in a cupboard I was cleaning out.

There were more mosquitos this year than I remember
        ever seeing before.
A wet spring favored their breeding habits, but I suspect
that other factors, not yet clear, also contributed to their abundance.
About the middle of May they took over from the blackflies
and flung themselves on every warm-blooded creature they could reach.

All day the dogs were pawing them from their muzzles,
and I could at once strike several anywhere on my head,
which was like an inflated pincushion smeared with mud,
because they could get at me best when I was in the garden,
stuck to a spot, my hands trying to plant or weed or thin.

Now that they're gone, except for the few that appear
in the cool of the morning and again when the heat of the day is past,
I can calmly wonder about what possible purpose they serve.
A recent medical paper suggests that the anti-coagulant
the female mosquito is obliged to inject into her victim
is a necessary component in keeping animal blood

       from clotting too easily;
for it seems that coronary thrombosis is rapidly increasing
among people who are shielded by glass and air conditioning
from the bites of blood-sucking flies.

I tend to think that this, or something like it, is the case;
for I believe that all of life is interrelated —
that only out of ignorance do we fail to see the reason

       for any part of it.

For years I've been saying that I ought to make wine
from some of the fruit on the farm. This year I said it to Jerry,
after remarking, with a sigh, that the chokecherries were ripe.

I should have known better! Though himself no lover of alcohol,
that earnest nature took up the winemaking as a serious task.
The protesting girls were put to work gathering chokecherries,
his wife, just arrived to join him, was sent back for supplies,
and I — feeling I had carelessly roused an earth spirit
that must now be satisfied — was obliged to hastily read
what books and other literature I had on the subject.
Fumbling and laughing, we assembled in a large new plastic pail
some eight gallons of a sweet pinkish must. Then we covered the pail
with a transparent plastic sheet, and — not knowing where else to put it
where it might stay clean and undisturbed — hoisted it up
           on the landing
of the driving-shed loft, where it nestled in a mound of fragrant hay.
There it ferments merrily; and the neighbor's children,
newly come from the harvest fields with grain still in their pockets,
climb up to stare in wonder at the bubbling frothy mix.

When I go out in the morning each of the three dogs
touches its moist nose to my hand in silent acknowledgment
of the domestication that makes me the leader of their pack.
But there are evenings when they dimly remember their origin,
and moved by the fullness of the moon or the nearness
of some stray creature of the forest they throw back their heads

and give vent to the short barks and long drawn-out howl
of the wolf. In spite of my familiarity with the dogs
and the subservience I've come to expect from them,
that howling in the night causes me an inner shudder;
for it evokes man's ancient fear of the wolf,
abiding symbol of the monster that children thrill to in their tales.
    We humans seem to need a certain amount of terror —
despite fire and electricity, aren't we still afraid of the dark —
perhaps to satisfy our subconscious memory of the precarious struggle
that gave us birth. A friend of mine who is both scientist and poet
tells me that our every cell carries within it the entire history
of its evolution from the first obscure, mysterious stir of being.

    When I think about my ideal woman
I see her as caring, passionate, intelligent
and good to look at — and the last is important,
because I like to take pleasure in what I behold.
For my own eyes I try for beauty in everything I do,
whether I'm merely making a path through the forest
or piling firewood, or arranging furniture, or flowers, or food;
basically, the appearance of everything matters to me.
But that aside, I want someone open to magic moments,
when a feeling moves between us and we both melt:

someone, like me, for whom that's being most alive.

That happened, almost obviously,
when Jerry was leaving with Nicki and Amelia,
and with his very warm, attractive, lively wife,
with whom I'd developed a mutual, restrained affection.
We hadn't touched, but I felt that our friendliness
camouflaged a sense of feelings deeply shared;
so when we had all said our social good-byes I walked ahead
to the apple tree from where my last sight of her would be,
and when Jerry, as a tribute, slowed the car to a crawl
as they passed, I reached out and gave her a fresh golden apple,
and she, in her half-choked cry and smile, gave herself to me.

A huge, full, pale-yellow moon, patterned with warm shadows
like a smiling face, is rising above the eastern woods,
while to the west the fading orange sun is drawing in its fan of radiance
and calmly sinking through delicate drifts of pink and blue.
Small white clouds hover above the setting sun, their undersides aglow
with a fiery yet tender light, while on their backs there falls
the first soft silver of the moon. The sky darkens and stars appear;
down below, the shadows take on the deep rich greens and purples
that are seen on only such a night. Later, when the moon is high,
the brilliant stars sparkle in the sky and on the moving waters of the pond.

Standing on the bridge I stare a while longer, and then turn
and see my moonlit house. In pioneer days it was a grist mill;
the stone walls are two feet thick and built on bedrock,
and the mortar, stone hard, was made from lime
          burnt and slaked on the spot.
I left the lower storey as it was, but I rebuilt the wooden upper structure,
and discarded the wheel and inner works, and put in floors,
essential rooms, and simple furnishings. It's rude yet elegant,
and all I need. While Jerry's brood was here it was always alight.

Today, driving over to see my neighbor to the east,
I cross the phone company's arbitrary boundary,
which makes it a long-distance call to him,
though to the south I can call locally for forty miles.
He is my closest, yet at the same time distant friend.
His gentleness, his goodness, his rare purity of spirit
place him far from me: he even eases ants and spiders from his path;
untroubled, he can lie down at any time, on a grassy bank
          or heap of straw,
and innocently go to sleep.
    The wind is banging his barn doors when I arrive,
so I go at once to fasten them. From the top of the ramp
I can see him in the meadow, in the midst

of his Holstein-Hereford herd, intently bent over something
        on the ground.
I hurry down and prod my way through to him.

    A red calf is lying on its side, its body ballooned out horribly.
The herd circles it, trembling, their necks stretched out,
their noses sniffing death. My neighbor draws his pocketknife
and straightens the blade, then tries to stab it into the calf's side,
but the dull point bounces ineffectively.

    Desperately he turns the blade on edge and begins to saw with it;
soon he has sliced through the hide and then the body wall —
and the sharp hiss of escaping gas drowns out all other sound.
He cuts deeper and a pale greenish foam bubbles up.
The calf kicks out wildly, spasmodically;
its eyes are glassy, its tongue hangs from its mouth.
He seizes the jaws and blows with all his might into its throat,
then repeats that several times, but there's no response.

    The herd mills about uneasily; from beyond it his dog yelps sharply.
In the clouds lightning flickers, casting a bluish light
over the field, the dog and cattle, and we two mute men.
Quavering thunder rumbles around us.
When it has subsided my neighbor raises his head from the calf's side.
It's gone he says simply. *Another cattlebeast gone.*

When other boys went in for sports
I went in for girls. My every thought and act
was prompted by, centered on, tied to a fair young face,
and though crippled by shyness and poverty, cold, hungry,
confined to hushed patrolling past her house, or passionately
composing ardent lures in sweeping letters never sent,
I'd pause at every lush shop window and pick out
all that I would, if I just could, lavish on her,
and I'd vividly picture our future love, famed life,
prosperity. Oh, there was one quiet girl with green eyes
and pale freckles and long light brown hair upon whom I poured out
my whole being, for whom, in dreams, I gladly breathed my last;
but apart from once coolly passing me in the street,
with only a single, swift, incurious glance,
she scarcely knew I existed.

I'm never ready for the first red maple leaves.
Despite the seasonal signs I was still confident, a few days ago,
of ongoing greenness, but now there are scarlet sprinklings everywhere.
And this morning, after a particularly frosty night, I woke

to see out my window a large patch of gold
        that had not been there before.
Soon afterwards, out walking, I saw ahead of me a red fox,
and then overhead, like some creature out of a fairy tale,
there slowly rose a great blue heron. Geese were flying yesterday,
the ragged formation honking like a pack of distantly baying hounds.
    Why am I moved by such things? I was drawn to the woods
at about age six or seven, out of a deep sense of necessity,
because a Yiddish refrain I heard often then —
Ohn a haim un ohn a lahnd: Without a home and without a land —
had made a deep impression on me, had in my childish mind
translated itself to mean that a man might at any moment
be thrust out of whatever comfort he temporarily enjoyed,
and, to survive, had to be able to cope with the primeval.
At first I was scared, and forced myself to fish and hunt,
and to sleep alone among the night creatures,
but gradually I came to love that world, and that love
has given me moments of pleasure ever since.

Mellow, succulent and sweet, the corn seems almost too good to eat.
Surrounded by prickly leaves of squash, which keep raccoons away,
the tall stalks stand in simple majesty. The Incas built an empire
on this plant; fresh or dried, it sustains us in ways still not understood:

there's something in the milky juice that eludes the measurements
of test-tube men. Its more obvious properties, though,
      have long been used:
maize, as most of the world calls it, yields sugar, oil, starches, gums,
and for cattle the whole green growth is a favorite food.
Few plants are so completely useful; one day, when the earth
has been stripped of all its easy pickings, industry's scarce resources
will come from fields of castor beans, milkweed, and corn.
Then we might also remember the playful possibilities of this good grass,
and like the Indians plait from its husks straps and mats, masks and dolls.
    I recall, before the days of cancer cares, rolling the dried silks
in a piece of leaf for a surreptitious smoke, and later,
trying to be casually grown up, stuffing aromatic tobacco into the bowl
      of a corncob pipe.

    About that time, when I was a strapping eighteen,
a poised, pretty woman perhaps eight years older than me
came for a visit to the immigrant farm family
with whom I lived and for my keep worked hard as a hired hand.
She'd escaped her war-torn homeland by marrying, perforce,
an older man: a sly, shrewd banker who'd obtained, through bribery,
a visa valid only for a man and wife, and now
svelte in silks and fur, she seemed to have all her heart might want,

except a child, and — from her wistful look . . . a little love.
  Lusty, amorous, I was eager to supply the last,
but she was put off by my mute, muscled, pushy, ogling passes,
was offended by that crudeness, not, as at first I thought,
by my supposed lower class. Finally I offered
to read to her, and with the pretext of it improving
her English we'd sit after supper on the orchard bench
and in a low voice I plied her with the most persuasive love poems
in the language. She'd sigh, sometimes blush. When it got too dark
we'd walk awhile, and on the last evening of her stay
she took my arm, and when I stopped, looked searchingly at me
and wept, and leaned her head against my chest, and I held her —
tenderly: by then this felt too delicate to disturb. Ah, but
soon after, when I was already keen on someone else,
I received by mail a plain-wrapped parcel that proved to be
a slim snowy book of Shakespeare sonnets and selections,
in which this pain-racked cry alone was underlined in red:
    My only love sprung from my only hate!
    Too early seen unknown, and known too late!
So my every grasping carefree look, word, touch had been a seed,
dreadfully grown rank into a dear woman's agony.

Man alone has mastered the monotony of producing identical objects;
in the rest of nature no two of anything are quite alike.
The goats give milk out of teats with small openings, and teats
from which the creamy goodness flows at the merest pressure
      of the fingers.
Each of the does has a distinct personality; indeed I often name them
after women they remind me of. No two leaves are the same,
or clouds, or drops of water, or dragonflies.
Each crumb of soil teems with an incredible variety of tiny animals,
not one of which is exactly like another; each human carries
      on and in his body
a greater number of creatures than there are people on this earth.
And even the most precisely manufactured things that meet every test
of uniformity — can they be said to be really the same,
when the electrons of their atoms display individual characteristics?

On this splendid, sunlit, rain-washed Sunday morning,
in the glistening grass, I found the stiff shining body of the big male dog.
A few spots of blood on the tawny chest, a drain of blood
      around the teeth,

and his tongue twisted under him; all other injuries internal.
Uncomplaining his nature was, and so his end; bloody footprints
  on the porch
showed that he had waited there until the last, and then
  had quietly gone out
and lain down in the grass. A large, friendly, affectionate, foolish dog;
may he return easily to the soft earth in which I laid him.
 As for the liquored-up Saturday-night buck who deliberately
ran him down — I would as willingly have buried him!
  He was much more an animal.
But then, the indifferent earth doesn't distinguish;
that same, last empty silence swallows all distinctions.

 All our rituals of death are for the living,
to alleviate our knowing that, inescapably,
we are next. And yet, my loss of someone deeply loved,
a woman who moved me as no other ever had,
has left, even after many long years, a feeling
that in my abiding love for her I am already dead.
But she, in me, is very much alive: impatiently,
but with her usual, amused, remembered grace,
she awaits the recognition of a mirrored face.

The Solomon's seal is rampant now. There are great red slashes of it
in the woods, the clustered berries forming sheets more brilliant
than any but the brightest leaves. And all around is an explosion of color:
white baneberry, red belladonna, blue cohosh, dark blue dogwood,
and the winy, deep red, almost black, chokecherries. How blue the sky is!
Sunlight is never so brilliant as on orange leaves.

Human lives too become decorated in autumn,
draped with ribbons, jewels and honors for work well and faithfully done.
What nonsense it all is! Who in his heart doesn't know how far he's failed,
how subtly the goal has eluded him. We have a desire to reach
for what can never be attained. I wonder if other forms
      share this dissatisfaction —
if each fading flower and drying leaf feels the same futility.

Tilling under the garden residue,
I notice that weeds do not at once begin to wilt,
even in bright sun: the cool air naturally sustains them.
Loneliness does that for memories. I recall women I have loved,
and cling to each in fond conversation and a close embrace,
and then, when I'm asleep, one sometimes joins me in an airy bed.

It's a kind of mental masturbation, and is embarrassing,
but it peoples the day, and fills a bit the aching emptiness,
and lets me feel I'm still a loving person and a social being.
Yet, induced by the falling leaves, there are times like this
when make-believe, conscious or not, collapses — leaving me hollow,
and baring my misery, and my still deeper, spreading despair.
Then it seems without purpose that I write, or even move,
flex my body, touch and taste, hear and smell, or see, or breathe.

The hillsides have grown thin; gone are the gorgeous coverings,
evergreens are prominent again. Gray clouds fill the sky;
it begins to rain; a sudden gust of wind scatters yellow leaves.
The rain thickens and becomes snow; now it is snowing heavily.
But the sky lightens once more; a whitish glare muddles through
        the clouds;
the downfall shrinks to silvery slivers. Suddenly tiny birds appear.
    Finally the rain stops. A faint glow outlines the treetops;
the ponderous clouds move on, exposing a patch of blue;
and a single sunray backlights the trembling water beads
        that bejewel the branches.

My fondest memory of an exquisite image
is of fresh, crisp escarole in a cracked wooden bowl.
It's on a cedar table set for two, on one side
of a wide, big-windowed room on the second storey
of what had once been a large, high-society home.
And on the far side of the flat, near the small bathroom,
stands an easel, and in the bay, below the casements
overlooking the lawn, lies a low bed disguised by day.

At that table we had our sensuous May suppers
of wine, bread and cheese, with salads of sliced tomatoes
and lettuce, and the escarole — as new to me then
as the sweet lovemaking I was soon introduced to
in that soft bed. She was gentle and kind and comely,
with long orange hair to her waist, and when I awoke
beside her in that book-lined room, where her canvases
were stacked against the cases — she was sometimes well paid
for the portraits she painted, but also liked to work
on her own subjects and themes — I, who was still eighteen,
felt privileged beyond all accounting for. *Why me?*
I begged, and she said, smiling *Because it's spring, and you
have broad shoulders and a thick neck.* Which was tongue-in-cheek,
because for her it became real love; and I, a boy,
bunglingly betrayed it. I cast eyes on a cute girl

who briefly seemed enchanting, and when, cured, I came back,
I found my dear lady's door barred to me. Bewildered,
I called to her, and she opened it a crack and said:
You can't come in— I'm married—. I left dejected, crushed,
knowing I had caused a possible catastrophe.
I've wondered if that abrupt marriage made her happy,
but whatever, I hurt her, and that still bothers me.

I go out into the luminous night,
and lift my eyes to the dark horizon of tree-fringed hills,
and then to the dancing band of moonlit clouds,
and then to the moon itself, pure and whole, and only then do I notice
the sharp clean streak of vapor trail slicing the sky,
and I'm suddenly reminded that man's been up there, and has walked
       on the moon,
and has already littered space with tons of metallic junk;
and I realize I'm gazing upwards through veils of history,
and feel myself rapidly shrinking into a remote residue of the past.

The ice on the pond forms and recedes, forms and recedes,
as cold and warm air masses battle for power over it.
It's like good and evil; the one is never in control
without the other threatening to undo it.
   When I look up from the pond at the starry sky
I find God a limiting concept; but I guess it is useful in human affairs,
where it provokes all the evil and encourages all the good
          we are capable of.

For my part I'm apprehensive about messiahs —
religious, political or psychological:
any prophet, expert or seer who promises certainty —
and I'm quite wary, despairing, of any woman pledged to one.
   So I've first tried to know women I might make love to;
for with the possibility of pregnancy ever present,
and most loath to have her then faced with a painful choice,
I'd pause in my approach and, duty bound, ask myself
if I was bindingly prepared to be the father of her child,
and if I couldn't commit to that, I'd back away.
   Oh, for the right woman I would take on anything;

but not, please, against impossible expectations —
nothing can satisfy all a believer expects,
because life, I fear, is infinitely more complex.

    It's not yet the middle of the month and we're knee deep in snow,
while the radio weather men, in gloating tones,
report dry conditions to the south, some wisps of snow here and there,
occasional flurries off the big lake to the west,
and even an inch or two in the snow-belt areas!
Why have they not placed a weather station here? *Untypical*...
No doubt: it would upset the generality of their forecasts.
The elevation of this small plateau makes it a trip device
for releasing the immense quantities of moisture
that the cold northwest winds pick up when they cross
the still-warm waters of the great wide bay.
Driven upwards from the beaches, heavy with vapor,
their crystals swelling as the air gets colder,
the snow clouds seem to reach their limit of retention
        right above the farm,
and in a celestial paroxysm that sometimes seems never ending
they let loose their enormous load of frozen fluid —
which falls, and falls, and falls on us.

Only in the north can one see clearly the anatomy of trees.
In warm lands if you ask children to draw a tree they'll start with
a mass of foliage; here they always begin with the trunk and limbs.
 Bare trees show a lean sturdiness and grace;
they make the glossy evergreens look fat and overdressed.
All reach for the sky, but some with the delicacy of a lacy fan
and others as if they wanted to grasp the air.
They awe me; yet I see that they are simply giant plants
struggling to survive like everything else.
Winds shape them, worms chew leaves and bark, viruses silently
       work within.
In the woods you can see them at all stages of life:
young and fresh, becoming mature, gnarled and old,
and those that have been toppled, broken or split by storms.
 The casualties become my firewood.
But when they're hung up on other trees it's often tricky
       to bring them down:
I can influence but never completely control their fall.
Woodsmen call those *widowmakers*, and I try to remember
that there won't even be a widow looking for me.
 Some years I manage to cut a few loads while the forest is dry,
and it's a sensuous treat, stepping with leather boots on crisp leaves
and smelling sawdust, moss, mushrooms and mould.
But usually I leave it too late, and then I'm slipping in snow,

skidding out the logs with tractor and chains, and unavoidably
getting soaked and cold. That's sensuous too,
but mainly in retrospect, with a warm mug in my hands
and my stockinged feet up near the heat.

I'd like to put my arms around a woman —
any woman. It wouldn't matter now if she was short or tall,
smart or dumb, old or young. Or even beautiful. As it is,
      I feel incomplete.

In a general way I'm seeing the unity of life
as I've never seen it before. In the last few years the lines between
earth and plant, plant and insect, insect and animal, animal and human
have become increasingly blurred, until they've virtually disappeared.
I have even let go the idea that there are two kinds of humans —
men and women; I now think there is basically one, and that
      only sketchily known.
Then what is all this life? What's this fantastic planet,
in which everything is alive, and related, and incredibly complex?

What is that endless universe, on whose near reaches our understanding
falls away? I suspect it is all one, from the slightest stir of any nucleus
to the infinite expanses of space.

Somewhere out there, you'd think, there'd be
just one, who if she knew me, knew me well, would helplessly
be moved by it. And I by her, if I could somehow uncover
the storehouse of her thoughts, and needs, and dreams.
Every person is a mine of hidden riches, with at most
a hint — sometimes in the eyes, or in their smile —
of what is there; but it's buried under many levels of fear,
and then, no one is free: there are other hopes, friends,
family — all the prior claims that usually come between.
But I, driven, now indulge in childish reveries
of finding, say, a lost skier or a stranded motorist
and bringing her into the warmth of this open fire,
and of my affection; how fine that would be,
and how unlikely, how desperate it is.

A few minutes ago I went out to the workshop to get some tools;
turning back from shutting the door I was struck still by the sight
    before me:
long lines of warm light streaming onto the snow from the lamp
    on the porch,
and porch and house and lamplight nestled in banks and hills
sculptured in a thousand shades of dewy silver, all shining softly
    in the moonlight.
Sky and snow alike were glowing; the river, usually dark, rippled
with glimmering movement, and even the deepest shadows
    were faintly luminous.
    It's all so far beyond the range of film or canvas,
        it makes me humbly grateful for my eyes.

    Solitude begets a habit of silence,
especially about the small happenings of the day.
Sometimes I point out something to the dogs,
but they are so thrilled to hear me speak that they prance and bark,
paying no attention to what I say.
    The goats seem to listen with more care,

but only to learn whether my words might mean more grain, or molasses,
or some other tidbit they are interested in.
The horses want only to be fed and let out to roam;
the sight of a saddle makes them turn away.

   Yet once in a while, driven to behold a human face,
I ride the mare over to hospitable neighbors on the west,
but the visit always has a hearty emptiness,
and the horse, skittish on the way out,
fidgets at her tether, impatient for the return trip.

   Except for a few cards I receive,
none of the midwinter festivals touch me here;
but hearing references to them on the radio,
along with the familiar songs,
deepens my sense of being alone.

On an unexpected greeting card, a very young woman has written:
There's an underlife which lies quietly beneath all things. As a child
I accepted it without question, but with age it becomes harder and harder
to trust the feeling that nothing is as it seems.
She adds that I am about the only person she can say this to.

   She's written this because inadvertently I must have said or done
something to move her, as she moves me now, but I can't openly respond.
A gentle, pretty girl, the daughter of a cartoonist and painter,

I would take her in an instant if age and attitudes didn't stand between.
But what would her parents say? What would she feel, once she was over
her first rapture and fear? Yet it might do us both so much good —
the fulfilled recognition, the brief moment of joy, however much
we paid for it in lingering pain. No, there's too much against it,
most of all my imagining that she's what I want.

    I'll think about her for hours, and then write politely;
because I know better, it's up to me to let it pass.

    Today the cold weather has given way to freezing rain.
The snow surface slowly dissolves;
the lacy edges of river ice are losing their crispness;
dark patches appear on the hillside where springs are flowing.
There are no shadows: snow and sky merge,
and trees stand like black lines on a grayed ground
that is neither blue nor green,
but subtly compounded of both.

A mistress of mine used makeup magically,
used it so well I rarely knew that she had any on.
I once mentioned that admiringly, and she said *Less is more*—
which was more or less her rule in most non-carnal things.

She was an English, blue-eyed, peaches-and-cream blonde,
a true unbleached blonde both in what is commonly hidden
and in the high-swept coiffure with which she crowned, for me alone,
her graceful head: she'd arrive looking like a duchess.
It gave her pleasure, she said, to put up her hair,
so that at just the perfect molten moment of desire
her deft pull of three key pins would send it all cascading down,
followed swiftly by her dress and rings and underthings.

She applied the same style to dealing with emotions,
talking softly in a warm fond way until we both felt good,
and then, in melodious English much more cultured than mine,
she'd tell me clearly and firmly what was on her mind.

She said *I'd rather be a mistress than a wife,*
because men, I've seen, are much nicer to their mistresses.
She liked that term, which troubled me, and was hardly even apt;
for we were both unmarried, and otherwise quite free,
and lived apart, and had our own pursuits and friends —
and I, then fairly poor, was rather often in her debt.
Yet twice each week, without fail, in keeping with our standing tryst,
she came and cooked a great meal, and stayed for morning tea.

I think for her the term symbolized her total giving,
as now, too late, it stirs my gratitude and deep regret.

The thaw, interspersed with freezing days, has reduced
the weight of snow
on the roofs, and that's fine, but it has glazed the road and deepened
the crust on the snow. On the steel driving-shed roof the layer of snow
has slid part way down and curled under, like a sheet of limp white toffee,
but when it falls it will pack into a hard breastwork
that I'll have to attack with a pickaxe and shovel to get the tractor out.
The horses, when they aren't slipping on the ice, crash through the crust
with mud-tinged hooves; rabbits and foxes, forced to skitter
on the surface,
leave earth-inked trails that might have been printed on some giant press.
The dogs, excited by the apparent nearness of prey, slide and flounder
in their haste to run it down, but they soon come back with empty jaws,
panting, frustrated, and pleased.
Only the other house remains pristine, the approach to it
undisturbed.
I built it long ago, with all the conveniences a woman might want,
thinking it would be needed if I ever married, but it has stood empty
ever since.
I do only what's required to keep it in repair.

Splitting firewood is for me a winter chore;
I do it on days that are dull. The swings of the sledge
liven things up, and the result is certain and quick.
Wood dried a year is already half split — the cracks show
where it wants to part. You put in the wedge, give it a whack,
and the piece divides with a satisfying sound.
But woods vary. Maple splits clean; elm clings, and sometimes
beech and cherry do. It depends on how the tree has grown,
or if it was heavily branched. Yet a twist or a knot in a sculptor's hands
might become a heroic head; Eskimos say the life is in the stone,
that they only let it out. And don't we each create in a dramatic way,
acting our self-made role? Playwrights all, we revise in thought
the scenes we see, and infuse them with what we feel.
Largely, our lives are the dramas we make in our minds.

Queen of the forest,
white birch is really too lovely to burn,
and I never fell one without deep regret.
But inescapably we humans are beasts of prey, we live by killing;
countless living plants and creatures are slaughtered to sustain us;
each of us cuts a swath of death throughout our life.

Yet the beauty of the birch isn't easily ignored.
The alabaster bark retains its grace; even as the split wood
      admits the flames,
the shred that slipped away curls itself enticingly.

For me, the beauty of all the earth
is but a reflection of women. Not of course
at conscious times, but when a child-born feeling
overcomes my mind, then the forms of hills, valleys, trees,
flowers, sea and sky are their eyes, brows, mouths,
hair, bodies and juices, and I see the whole world
beyond the curved swelling of my mother's breast,
or from the warm soft bosoms of all the women
I have ever been with. Oh, I well know that
women can be base, hating, greedy, murderous —
like men; but they're also able to give birth,
and they carry that extra burden gallantly.
They've given me the best of life: wonder, bliss,
all my basic standards of beauty.

There's a convergence of small springs
where the hillside slope is broken by a tiny terrace.
A slight rise there checks their flow, the way a highway does
when it's pushed across a valley on a piled-up mound.
Slowed to a seep, the springs form a swampy spot
no broader than the river span — a deer could cross it in two bounds,
yet it has in miniature all the conditions of a marsh.

Bulrushes grow there; and now their stiff stalks,
topped by the fuzzy brown flower spikes, are sticking out of the snow.
And among them run the casual prints of the raccoons
who continue to sleep under the roof of my writing cabin,
though I've tried everything short of murder to keep them out.
The cabin, incidentally, also serves to keep surface water
out of the stronger spring I use. Below the floor, underground,
this spring rises in a round well and then circulates through a reservoir,
in which the water is always flowing, always fresh.
Delicious water, it's pulled a long way by a pump,
and then sent under pressure to every building on the farm,
and up to outdoor troughs for the cattle and horses, and the goats.
I put a lot of work into this system and at first was very proud of it,
but with time it has settled indifferently into the natural order
        of the place.
The little marsh, which I can see from where I sit, also attracts birds,
and I've seen mink sliding from it on their bellies down the slope.

Here it's only the free creatures who play in snow.
I don't own skis, and snowshoes I use only when I must.
Sleds I keep for moving things about.
But there've been moments when I've stretched out on my back
and caught the falling flakes with open mouth, ready —
at least until I froze! — to enter into the all-encompassing,
       icily warm dream
of white.

   The February sun is warm; despite biting air, crisp snow,
and massive ice on the river, its welcome heat caresses me.
Last night in a dream I was swathed in white, somehow disabled,
and the young woman on whom all my yearning centered
       was leaving me;
to keep her from going I reached out blindly —
my fingers caught her inner thigh; her kiss was moist and sweet.
   I envy Donald his Diane. The other house,
which I rented to them because of her fair face and form,
now doubly mirrors my loneliness.

Overnight it grew warmer, snow fell heavily,
and with morning light a clear cold returned.
Almost instantly it freeze-dried every laden bush and branch.
I called to the dogs and two bumps in the snow
        rose and shook themselves;
apart from their depressions and our tracks, the entire landscape
        was unmarred.
It was all such a perfect *winter wonderland* it looked ludicrous,
like a giant snow set; I walked about and wanted to laugh out loud.
    But I know there is measureless power in this placid display,
inherent violence in such an immensity of snow.
So I keep my amusement to myself, hoping the winter furies
        haven't noticed,
or don't mind.

Outside this sheltered valley there's another world.
This morning, in sunshine, when I was visiting a neighbor
        five miles away,
the wind rose.
    In his restrained, polite way he urged me to go at once or stay;

but confident in my four-wheel drive and the warmth at home,
I somewhat smugly lingered.
When I did go, cutting across the northwest wind,
I could still make out his barn and sheds,
but within a mile everything disappeared in a whirlblast of white.
I realized then the seriousness of the storm, and would have turned back,
but the road, already drifted between high banks, was too narrow
      to allow it,
and I could no more see behind me than ahead.

    I stopped and waited, four minutes, perhaps five,
until suddenly the wind dropped for an instant and I saw a hydro pole.
Then I drove on, steering by the poles,
forcing the jeep through axle-high drifts that reached across the road.
Until one refused to yield.

    Taking a shovel and tying down my parka hood, I stepped into
      the screaming wind.
The drift was higher than the bumper, but only three or four yards broad;
I set to work to clear a way.
The wind tore at my clothes and mitts, the driving snow stung like sand;
after a few dug paces I could no longer see the jeep.
By the time I'd shoveled through the drift, its first part
      had almost filled in,
but I regained the driver's seat, put the vehicle in gear, and bucked ahead.
There was wet weight on my cheeks and lips: the softened snow,
but I had nothing with which to wipe it off.
Then I was stopped again.

    I got out, determined to shovel through once more,

but the wind and snow seemed equally eager to prevent it.
Before I'd shoveled my own length my hands and face
        were becoming numb,
and I could feel the cold crushing my toes.
And then a sudden maverick gust rent the white and in a forward glimpse
I saw no road — this drift went on and on, beyond my sight.
But in that same instant, before the snow-lashed sky closed in,
        I saw a house.
    Diagonally across the fields, it was less than a quarter mile away,
and luckily I knew who lived there: a father, mother, and two grown sons.
I shut off the engine, lowered my head, and plunged
        into the mounded snow.
I thought I might strike wire; I couldn't remember whether that field
        was fenced,
but when I had struggled through the chest-deep ditch
the snow leveled off below my waist and I could move slowly ahead.
Now I was facing directly into the wind — a blessing in its way,
because it gave me the right direction,
yet unendurable whenever I raised my eyes.
    A dark mass appeared vaguely to my left, and only with difficulty
did I recognize it as a clump of cedars that grew at the end
        of the long lane;
the house was farther left of it — but for those trees
        I would have missed it.
    I found my way to the outer door, thumped on it, but got no answer.
I turned the knob, the door swung in,
and I stumbled into the dark shed and over to the kitchen door.

It opened before me: one of the sons had heard;
beyond him in the room his father and mother stood.
But all three faces were so grave, so shocked, so set in disbelief,
that I thought: *Some tragedy has taken place— where is the other son!*
I didn't understand until the mother broke the silence.
Bringing a soft towel, she said *Sweet Jesus, you're all over ice!*

Hours later, when the wind had died and a thin moon was rising,
the father kindly insisted on sending his two sons
— the other had been upstairs on his bed, reading a comic book —
to open the road with their large tractor and blower,
and I, warmed, fed, restored, was easily restarted on my way.
They went ahead of me to the nearby east-west road,
           which had hardly drifted,
and I've driven here without further incident,
grateful for the ungrudging helpfulness of farmers,
and glad to be again between the sheltering hills of home.

To have a home, where there's warmth and a woman,
sometimes seems to me the greatest single joy.
It's complicated, of course; no two people
can combine their ways without some conflict,
but I feel there's an essential sweetness
and fulfillment about family life —

about an evening lamp lit by someone else,
a meal prepared for and eaten in common,
a wide-enough bed with a warm body in it.
Sentimental slush? — perhaps suggested by
the heavy silence of my bachelor house?
I think not; I think there's something satisfying,
basic, alive, about sharing goods and powers,
about saying seriously, lovingly, *ours*.

One of my great pleasures, after a hard and sweaty week,
is to bathe completely, wash my hair, clean and trim finger and toe nails,
and put on an entire change of clothing, each piece of which
          is newly laundered
and smelling fresh. I like to do it at week's end;
for my washing is as much a ritual as the day of rest. I like the idea
of a day of contemplation, in which to think about past mistakes;
when I walk about instead of working it gives me a sense
          of order and repose.
They knew what they were doing, those ancient Hebrews,
          with their code;
after all this time it still satisfies a deep-felt need in us.
An orderly life, I think, frees one to create
without wasting effort in superficial ways.

Indeed, most other problems
can be met with initiative, talent and energy,
but loneliness gnaws away like an insatiable worm,
silently sapping everything I try to say.
I feel disintegrated, like I'm drowning in my mind.
I cling to rationality as to a raft, to words
as signals of my soul.

The pebbled road is dry and gray beneath a soft gray sky.
Brown patches show along its sides — the first time in months we've seen
bare earth. As the dogs and I approach, five crows rise slowly
      from a carcass
flung up on the snow: a young raccoon, its stomach torn open,
its nose and eyes bloodied. The dogs, who probably killed it, turn away,
eager to continue the walk. The season of life begins.

2

TOGETHER

I've met her! An accidental meeting in the city —
spontaneously arranged by mutual friends not seen for many years.
You must come! they said to her, and separately, about an hour later,
the same to me; perhaps by then they were bent on kindly mischief.
  What a creature! Beautiful, vivid, irrepressible —
I instantly recognized that it was she.
Unmarried too; when I noticed she wore no ring she said
    I'm a good runner!
and I understood she had been grasped by many men but never held.
I'm a child of Hitler! she cried, and the holocaust arose and shattered me.
All this in minutes; then it was time to go:
our hosts were hurrying to a concert.
  Esther went I knew not where,
but I carried the essence of her away with me; and now,
driving home, though it's dark, it seems to me there's sunlight
    on the snow!
I won't ever pretend to be rational again.
Where does she live, how can I reach her?
When my bewilderment has passed I must begin an earnest pursuit.

The river has broken through the millpond ice —!
Pushing ahead of it a crest of yellow foam,
the current inched its way towards the dam,
and then suddenly swept the final shrunken bar over the streaming edge.
Now a lively dark gash cuts across the white plane of the pond,
and the water, crashing over the dam,
splashes against the basestones of my house.
    I suppose Esther will want the other one —
it has closets, extra bathrooms, a terrace and lovely views;
but perhaps she won't want me.
Though she's had much to do with men,
she's still quite young, maybe twenty-five or six —
the gap between us might appear unseemly to her friends.
And there's the way I live, on home-grown food, with an uncertain income,
and nothing in the bank — it's very little to offer such a prize.
Nonetheless I won't pretend;
I've written asking her to come and see me as I am.

Three days of clear sunlight have etched a skewbald pattern
on the southeast slopes. The dogs, still in their winter coats,

flop on the remaining snow: the bare ground is already
      too warm for them.
On the other side of the valley the shaded hillsides
      dimly gleam with moisture;
under the crumbling crust a ubiquitous tide is seeping
      through the wakened grass.
The river is in flood — *a mighty torrent* seems its apt description.
Partridge and chickadee are getting drunk on swollen belladonna berries;
and moss, under the potent sun, is turning a vivid green.
Don and Diane — whom I now bless! — have come out of their house,
and warmed, dazzled, almost stunned, they stand and stare vacantly
      around them.

    Their new cat has had kittens. A stray they found wandering in town,
starved, half wild, she quickly adapted to regular meals
and a secure place to sleep. Small, hardly more than a kitten herself,
we thought she had aborted the day she gave birth —
      nowhere were any kittens to be seen.
Today, two weeks later, Diane found them, four of them,
in the darkest corner under the worktable in her garage,
where the young cat had dragged a tattered towel for their bed.
Instinctively a devoted mother, the cat is reluctant
      to let us play with them;

she spits and growls when our fingers come too close.
The father is probably one of the two barn toms, though
        I haven't seen either
since the young cat came; they take off at the slightest sign of spring.
Or if not one of them, it's some tom from miles away;
they can pick up the heat scent on the faintest breeze.
Indeed there was a lot of yowling weeks ago, and the dogs
        were busy barking
half the night. Under our noses these creatures live a life of their own,
in a world that wakens when we sleep; they deign to let us feed them,
and are tolerant of our need for love.

    This is the Sunday I asked Esther to visit,
and so far there's been no sound or sign from her. Uneasily,
suppressing fearful fantasies, I slowly dial her number.
It rings hollowly, hauntingly, over and over. Then suddenly:
What? Good morning—! she sings out, as if in the middle of a sentence.
Good morning I say. *Am I interrupting something?*
No . . . why? she says. *I was just looking at the sunshine.*
A good sign! I think, fast becoming heady, as if hearing her voice
was close to having her. *It's me* I say. *From the farm. Today's the day.*
I know she says, and her tone turns firm, curt, direful: *How are you?*
Fine I reply. *Are you coming?* There's a long pause, which gets grim.

No she says; then adds: *I don't think so.* The last tells me it's pure choice.
Oh I say, too dismayed by this disaster to quite believe it:
I try to mouth something funny, but can't; then my hopes collapse.
Yet I add, mumbling: *Only . . . uh, it's too bad about the goose.*
What? she cries. *What goose?* And I explain that a neighbor
had given me half a large goose, which I'd kept frozen,
but that has been thawing since last night. *Oh . . .* she says,
and I can hear the struggle in her silence. *Well,*
she goes on at last *I guess we can't waste the goose.*

The house is spotless, and I've scraped the stables,
and am spreading soft beds of cleanly-gleaming straw.
There's something sensual about the fresh bedding;
I'm being roused merely by relating it to that exciting girl,
and by the potent, thrilling thought that she's now well started
         on her way.
I've just time to finish chores, baste the goose, shower and change;
and then perhaps be reading by the pond when she arrives —
I want her to see that we're civilized here in the hinterland,
and, given some leisure, manage to nurture values of the mind.
With these thoughts I'm rolling out the last barrowful of manure
when the dogs, torn from its smells, begin their typical barking
at an as-yet-unseen approach, and around the corner

comes a faded, flesh-colored compact car. On seeing me,
the driver slows it, and the dogs, thinking they have done that,
now boldly attack its front bumper, by bits giving ground
until they've brought the beast to a full stop where I stand.

    Oh God, it's her! — as I knew, before, it had to be.
She half smiles, open-mouthed, both shyly and in satisfaction
at having found her way. *I was worried about getting lost,*
she says *so I started early.* And caught me in dirty coveralls
and spattered boots, still absently holding the heavy reeking barrow.
I set it down and step closer: she's all I remembered —
even imagined! My fever over her being here
robs me of all inner poise, and more gruffly than intended
I say *Drive down to the bridge, and then pull up at the garage—*
I'll get rid of this and join you right away.

    When I go hurrying down she's out of the car
and by the flower bed, staring at the double white narcissus.
I don't know if their surprising, exquisite perfume has reached her,
but she seems rapt, distracted, so I don't intrude. We both stand
        quite still.
After a moment she looks up and, without speaking, walks to the bridge,
trailed by the transformed dogs, who've already sensed her status.
She leans against the railing and looks down at the river,

and out over the pond. Swallows are swooping across it,
trout rise and splash, sunlight glitters on the rippling water.
In contrast to me, the place is looking its best, and its beauty and hers
seem, suddenly, to belong together. Inwardly, yes, I yield to that:
it's all hers; yet I don't move, having hard won my right to stay.

She turns then, looks beyond me, and says, gamely *Is that the house?*
I nod, and mutely follow her down the worn flagstone walk,
moving ahead only to open the door to the porch,
and then, past the woodpile, the formal one. She steps inside
and stops there,
glancing around the living room. Across it, the stately French windows
stand a storey above the river; she can see spume, hills, sky.
Now she regards the stairs at her feet and slowly descends them,
her high heels making little toc-tic sounds on each varnished step.
Behind her, I begin to smell the rich garlic-spiced gravy
in which the goose is steadily simmering, gently moist-roasting the meat.

Esther pauses at the lower room's center post and does a slow pivot,
her eyes silently taking in the white unpainted walls,
the oak plank floor, black iron stove, broad teak dining table,
and, in passing, the open doorway into the tidy, workmanlike kitchen.
Then they come decisively, and with a hint of covenant, to rest on me.
Head held high, she says *I don't cook, and I don't clean.*

She eats, though — our early dinner is going splendidly.
For once I've got all of it right: the savory goose, rice, corn, salad,
and deep-red chokecherry wine are all delicious. And sitting with me,
her hair loose, her beauty and warmth radiating through the rooms,
driving out the loneliness, I feel she only needs to be,
and that's enough; at least for now. But . . . curious, perhaps pushing
my luck, I ask her if she's glad she came. *You know I am* she says.
Then why were you so reluctant? She looks at me and says *It was your letter.*
The first page was so romantic I almost swooned, but then I turned it over
and you said I couldn't smoke! Jesus I thought— nuts! To hell with that,
and with him! Who does he think he is? And when you called this morning
I got angry all over again. But I haven't yet seen a cigarette,
and she was smoking heavily when we met. *With me,* I say

      it's not the act—
mine isn't a moral stance— it's the actual smoke. It very soon gives me
a headache, and I can smell it in the house for days.

      She regards me solemnly
and says *I see . . .* And stops eating while she assesses that.

She wanted nothing when she first arrived,
so we walked, and I showed her the bank barn and stables,
the driving shed and, from a distance, the other house:
with Diane, agog, watching from a window; and then we went
along the river, where Esther kicked off the boots I'd lent her
and leapt barefoot from rock to rock, till she waded in to examine
blooming clumps of watercress, marsh marigold, and mint.
        I reached out once
to steady her, but quickly withdrew my arm unseen, realizing
she didn't need it, and afraid of playing the masterful male;
primarily I wanted this with us to seem, and truly be, unforced.
Afterwards we wandered through the woods, past drifts of wild flowers,
        to the field
where the four horses were, who, seeing her — something different —
came sidling over, and nuzzled her, and she stroked and petted
and sweet-talked them, and they neighed and wheeled,
        pushed and pranced
as if they'd known and loved her all their life, leaving me
both impressed and, if anything, just a little jealous.
    With all that we missed lunch, came back to the house dry and starved
and started in on the wine, and now that we're hungrily having
second helpings we've had to open another bottle, which is,
I can see, her substitute for smoking.

We're out by the pond, quietly observing
the water striders at their arabesques. Esther blows faint rings;
she finally had to have a cigarette. Down to the waist
we're still in rosy light; and below, bathed in the shot-through shadows
spreading from the willows on the other shore, as the sun, still strong,
begins nestling into the western hills. I have our wine glasses
and bottle balanced on a rock, and once in a while we both sip.
The cool air carries a scent of the first blossoms, mingled now
      with smoke.
Esther stubs out; then, embarrassed, looks round for a place
      to drop the butt,
and seeing none, puts it in the pocket of her white silk blouse,
where it seems more gross, much, than it would anywhere on the ground.
It won't work . . . with this she says, frowning, and her face tells me
she means this whole scene, and the life that goes along with it.
We're silent. I can't argue against her ways. The risk widens . . .
when, reaching for the bottle, I have a sudden inspired flash:
I'll tell you what— I say *no cigarettes, but all the wine you want.*
She smiles, taking it as a joyful, half-serious joke; then shrugs.
Really, any kind— chokecherry, currant, grape— from anything we grow!
My fervor seems to affect her; her lips purse, she looks me in the eye
and holds out her hand, and I raise mine to grasp it. *Gorgeous,* I say,
with rash daring *you'll never regret this. No, I think not* she says,

and we shake hands like threatened traders who have come to terms.
I hang on, trying to say through my fingers what I feel;
we both tingle: it's the first time we have touched.

I want this woman so badly —
not just in bed, or for an affair, but, basically, for life
— that despite her evident enjoyment of what she's so far seen,
and the obvious small signs of commitment: her declaration
about cooking, and then the wine/smoking pact, I'm being careful
not to push or pull; like with a fish on the line I'm scared of losing her.
And she too seems much more restrained, low-voiced,
        than I suspect is usual.
We're lying on the hearthrug by the fire, wistfully a foot apart,
sometimes mutely studying the flames in between our bouts of talk.
It's grown dark and late, and remembering all we've had to drink
I wonder if she should be driving back tonight. But instead
I slyly speak of love, and say *What matters most to me*
is carrying a sense of the other throughout the day,
and then meeting and melting together at night. She breathes in,
as though she wants to gather and hold that, then looks at me
with warm eyes. *If I had such a love,* I say further
that woman would be my world, and I'd— we'd, defend it,

if need be, against all the outer one. She nods,
then laughs, in an odd way aptly, as if there were
more to this than I'm aware of.

Oh yes, the birds and I are singing,
and I'm supremely, giddily good-natured all these bright spring days.
Yet an even better time approaches, when Esther will be back,
when her small car — she'd just got it, bought it, from a girlfriend —
will come round the curve, sending the dogs into shrill delight
and me into an upsurge of instant utter bliss and abandon,
scarcely able to wait to get her, laughing and luscious, into bed.
    She stayed that first night, then the next, and it was all good;
we melded gently, joyously, as if formed to fit,
and, supreme test: we slept! — a deep, restful, dreamless sleep.
Mornings brought only more hours of mutual pleasure;
then it was time . . . I could hardly bear to have her leave —
but she had commitments in the city, and went back
to complete or put an end to them.

Esther has rolled up her sleeves and is baking bread.
She returned suddenly with a carton of olives and a can of yeast,
determined both to bring me into the world and to become
      a woman of the earth.
She had me grind some of our wheat on the small hand mill;
and her first loaf, though dense, had an excellent flavor.
Now she has two more in the oven, and seems pleased with their rising.
    I don't know whether this is a passing enthusiasm
or a prospect of things to come, but I keep my mouth shut
      and do as she says.

The wonderfully warm smell of baked bread
is still heavy in the house when we're in bed,
and I'm holding her, moist and sated, in my arms.
It's the moment before her mind trails her shutting eyes,
though a low, shaded lamp is still on — because for me
her beauty is an added element in making love.
Yet, happy as I am about how all this is going,
I feel the baking's moved us beyond being merely lovers,
and a more basic, intimate accounting is now required.

Slowly, benignly, I rotate round to sit at her side,
while she, startled, puzzled, peers at me through blinking lashes.
Esther, I say *don't be upset. But I must tell you something.*
You'll agree, I'm sure, that between us there shouldn't be secrets.
And I don't want you to have any nasty surprises . . .
She pulls back, her eyes widening in alarm, then anger:
You— you've got a wife and six kids! she cries.
No— I plead *please! No, it's, uh— a false tooth.*
What? My God, you have what?
A false tooth I repeat.
And I point to it: an upper incisor. *It was knocked out*
in a fight— when I was nine. A boy hit me with a broomstick.
Fool! she cries, and tangles in the bedclothes, laughing sudden tears.
Really! she sobs. *Such an idiot! Oh— come and kiss me—*
And, well I obey, till her crying stops.

She wants nothing to do with the other house. Moreover,
she's very much for women's lib — cheers when she hears
of couples breaking up — and thinks marriage a humiliating state.
To me? I say. We've been digging a rose bed by the pond.
She frowns and stares at the ground. *For my part,* I say,
trying not to provoke her *marrying doesn't matter. But don't you—*
Her distressed eyes dart this way and that, searching for escape,

then suddenly she turns — and dives into the pond!
I'm terrified: the water hasn't yet warmed, and some seconds later
there are still only widening ripples where she went in —.
 Panicked, I plunge after her, almost careless of
the icy shock, and, deep underwater, frantically feel about —
Not a thing — no one! *God, this can't be happening* I think;
and then, surfacing, I see her smoothly come up
nearly fifty feet farther on. She brushes back her hair, and though short
of breath, calls: *Marrieds do— such cruel things— to each other.*
The put downs— power trips— knifings— I don't want them!
And then she shakes, as if to cast that off, laughs,
 and lightly swims to shore.

 Her mother is now coming up the walk,
not waiting for Esther, who's moving things from the car.
I'd imagined — I don't know why — a portly matron,
but this woman is trim, attractive, and when she sees me,
smiles charmingly. My interest was roused days ago
when Esther mentioned that her mother often wonders
where she disappears to. I said *You haven't told her?*
And seeing a wedge, went on: *Well, why the mystery—*
invite her out. She shrugged doubtfully, but said she might.
 Earlier she'd told me it wasn't long

before we met that she stopped living with her mother,
mainly because the poor woman could seldom come home
without finding a man, and once, when she returned too soon,
a rumpled bed. Too, her mother would weep in despair
over all the spurned suitors: *Yes, laugh— you'll be spinstered—*
and I'll have ashes on my head! Now the lady's downstairs,
seeing if there's electricity, running water,
and whether, *dear God willing,* I really own the place.
 I'm going to gather a few flowers
Esther says, and whispers: *Don't let her take you for walks.*
A walk is her office, her control room— she'll strip you clean!
Then her mother comes up and says *Well, it looks quite nice.*
You'll show me around? So we're walking by the garden —
she's taken my arm — talking about her daughter's life.
And I say, firmly *It's true, I'm not the first—*
but I'll be the last. She stops— eyes wide with innocence,
hand on her heart, and says *I know nothing of such things—!*
But, wise man— you want me to sleep nights? Make her your wife!

 It's a case of common humanity I say.
Esther sighs and plays a silent violin: *I'll send her*
sleeping pills she says. *Oh, come on!* I say. *She doesn't have much else.*
Esther says she might consider that. Then she turns to the wine;

she wants more, and has plans for apple, carrot, and dandelion.
This morning, all melting, she sprinkled perfume on the wristband
      of my watch;
then a moment later, stung by my wry look, she turned angrily away.
When I embraced her she clutched my shirt front, and I asked her
not to crease it please; at that she became enraged, and cried:
You're a rigid, repressed, repulsive man! I was afraid I'd lost her,
when suddenly she smiled and said *You're no fun, but still the best.*

We're wading in the river, looking at fossils;
almost every second stone bears some imprint of shells,
or worms, or other life of long ago. *All this was once,*
I say *an inland sea.* Esther, half listening, nods.
Sure puts our petty issues in perspective I add.
She gives me a swift, ironic, sideways smile —
she knows I mean the impasse with her mother,
but she's also mocking my banality. *Don't worry about it,*
she says *it's between her and me.* Well — but the ultimate question is,
can this warm quicksilver ever be contained?

Wonder of wonders, Esther and I are married!
All at once she relented, but insisted on having the ceremony here,
behind the house, in the neglected flower garden, under the open sky.
And in that rush to respectability her mother put aside
       any uneasiness she had
about my age, my strange life, my lack of ready cash.
The guests, all family, arrived together, behaved with traditional gaiety,
and quickly went away, leaving me with a wife
       I'm just beginning to know.
Esther! Ardent and eager, she is precise about emotion,
vague about *facts*; a country and a continent are all one to her,
whereas she can define exactly the look in someone's eyes.
In the same way she seems to regard paper as belonging
       to the practical realm
and carries on a silent, grubby war against it;
no piece of it comes into her hands without being
       immediately crumpled,
smudged, torn — she has no patience with *fussy* tidiness.
She has taken our entire supply of maps — showing the route
       to the farm —
and squashed them into a side pocket of her purse,
where she carries them about like a heap of life preservers,
instantly flinging one to any friend who seems in distress.

Something happens to my bride in bed;
all her dash and verve abates, and she becomes supple
and accommodating, like a stroked cat, and then invariably
slips from sensuality into sleep. One night soon after
the wedding we both woke, still joined, and before resuming
spoke some whispered words that seemed to float on sighs.
I hadn't seen those narcissus since I was a child, she said
and a white-walled house has always featured in my dreams.
I entwined my fingers in hers, and felt her only ring
— we wear matched plain bands of gold, a gift from her mother —
and I said *Even now, when you have it?* She was quiet then,
but soon went on: *It's not quite real yet. It's so much you
that I still feel like I'm visiting, and this wonderful vacation
might soon end.* I wanted to say *It won't,* but I wasn't sure,
and instead sought security in burrowing into her welcoming body,
in immersing myself in her appeasing flesh.

Friends, friends, friends! she laughs
—just remember that you're mine. Fanatically I say.
Are they all women? Mmm . . . mostly she says. *Anyway, it'll give you*

a wider circle. No more living like a monk. Sex-mad monk I say,
hugging her. *The kind I like—* she kisses me *— but, seriously,*
darling, take a deep breath. They'll soon be at the door.
She told only her intimates about our marriage, but now
she's getting phone calls and letters from all over.
Well, I'll probably like your friends I say. *They're true family:*
freely chosen, bound only by affection, interest . . . and,
uh, a balanced exchange of favors. Fabulous she says.
But please try just talking to them.

Noisy, with tumbling steps, driven by hungry love,
Sheila is the first to arrive. Her laugh shakes the house.
Big boned, big breasted, she comes laden with cheeses and fruit,
filling the weekend with food and continuous talk. Completely rapt
in what she is saying, she follows at Esther's heels like a very large dog,
sweeping aside, without noticing, papers and petals caught in her wake.
Even at night she shakes in her sleep, as if straining to express
what she had failed to mention during the day.
Want it or not, I am included in her embracing warmth,
but at the outer edge, as yet untested, still largely unknown
to her and Esther both. They are members of a tight sisterhood
that doesn't easily admit outsiders.

Helen comes next, walking, perfectly at ease,
albeit her car is in the ditch and I must go and pull it out
with the tractor. She moved over too far to let the mail-lady pass;
then, no worse, coolly declined a lift and went on her way to us.
Is that the man? she says of me. Esther nods, and introduces me
as if I were the curious human feature of the place. Helen,
small and compact, regards me indifferently, and then turning to my wife
says she'd like to play her flute, which she has carried in its padded case
under her arm. They go off together to the house.

So you're married? Helen says when we three sit at lunch.
I look to Esther for assurance, but she impatiently goes on
with something else. They talk about Sheila, other friends, music,
books they want to read. Esther is so elated and alive
that I could simply sit and stare, uncertain yet
that this phenomenon is here to stay. But pride and planting take me out:
it's high time I put in carrots and kale. Lettuce, spinach, onions, peas
and the early root crops are well up; a third of the garden
is delicately frilled
with rows and beds of tender green.

Away from the women my resentment ebbs; Esther, I reflect,
is a guest I do not own. I look at the sunlight framing the hills
and think of all the energy I wasted in being alone, of the effort I made
just to keep sane.

Miriam — it's important to pronounce the *am* —
a solid lady, handsome, not to be trifled with,
flushes from the indignity of having to assert her claim:
You better treat Etti well, she hisses *she is mine!*
They call her Etti in their group, and she prefers that,
though Esther is a queen's name, and means a heavenly star.
And she is a star in the other sense; for notwithstanding
all the special virtues of her friends,
she alone has that instantly-appealing, exciting mix
of joyous warmth, beauty, and swift, passionate sentiment —
and a seemingly endless list of former lovers to attest to it.
Some phone her still, though she says she told them to desist;
I greet them coolly, but oblige, counting on her resolve
to confine my yielding to the instrument.

There's no escaping it — I am jealous;
I wonder whom she fantasizes when her eyes slide shut.
I asked her that, and she said *You silly man,*
when we are joined I have you outside, in me, and within,

so there are three of you I'm making love to all at once.
That's flattering of course, but does not ease my qualms:
I feel that there are unseen rivals all about.
Not that I doubt my worth — our daily pleasure is deep,
melting, eruptive, repeated until she feels she will explode,
and she loves it when I read to her, or when we talk,
and she is eagerly interested in all I think and do.
It's not any of those things; it's only that
when I'm so deeply moved by even her smile, or line of breast,
I don't see how others can help wanting her as much as I.

We've made a deal — it goes like this:
that because our marriage is primarily a bond of flesh,
we'll each have perfect freedom short of any carnal act.
As for adulterous feelings, we agree they cannot be suppressed,
but will rely on each other's tact not to show them overmuch.
I'm pleased with this; it frees her to go
where and when she wants, and, if it comes to that, with whom,
and frees me from worrying about her every minor step.
I know she'll lie — lies are mere conveniences to her,
but in all that's fundamental I have total trust.
There is in her a core that's absolute; she's given me

a place in it, among her secret griefs and fears,
and if I betray that, no matter how well I have behaved
I'll be cast out, and nothing else will be of any use.

Don and Diane have given notice;
it seems they've spent most of their savings on this country fling,
and now want to get back as soon as possible to the city.
For our part we're amicably letting them break their lease,
and because we don't like — no, really dislike — being landlords,
and though we've come to count on that much-needed extra cash,
we've decided not to hurry to rerent, but to let it ride
until we meet someone who might more suitably fit in.
   Not that the Ds were difficult, not at all; but we've found
that even one more person makes us a small community,
and now we'd prefer people with interests closer to ours.
Besides, though Esther was always fairly friendly with Diane,
I suspect she's relieved, perhaps quite pleased, to see her go;
even at a distance, Diane's polish and dressy perfection
were irritants I think my wife feels she can well do without.
Esther is, I've seen, just slightly uneasy with her own sex.

Well, I've got a gut sense of men, she answers me
but women— they play other games. No, I don't truly know them,
because from twelve on I was too busy being chased by boys—
some of them horny husbands with daughters older than me.
You matured early I say. She nods, modestly looking down.
I add, ruefully: *And some of those boys are still chasing you.*
She shrugs, her smile as much in sympathy with my discomfort
as by way of apology for her appeal. *And the sisterhood?*
Oh, that's different she says. *We're friends. We'd do almost anything*
for one another, no questions asked. She laughs. *Of course, we do ask,*
but, really, reasons and motives don't matter. In me, envy mixes
with, again, a feeling of being left out: *What about us?*
Wasn't it going to be the two of us against the world?
Sure, she says *but that doesn't make everyone else an enemy.*

We've quarreled seriously for the first time.
It began with a trifle; she wanted to hang a batik
Sheila had given her, and I said it wasn't art.
And that led to a long bickering about taste,
and I complained that she never dresses well or grooms herself.

And indeed she wears castoffs from her friends, or just clean rags,
and no makeup, hair often awry — she knows she's exciting nonetheless:
everything is carried by that wonderful body and beautiful spirited face.
    A big mistake, though, was my citing a particular woman
who has, like perfect pitch, impeccable, artistic taste.
That caused a choked, exasperated cry, then hot speechlessness . . .
which goes on yet. My wife is like that, I've noticed.
Any accidental cut or blow brings a sudden jarring roar of rage,
and when I rush over, trembling, thinking she's been badly hurt,
I get a curt *It's nothing!*, and those lovely shoulders turn away.
Pain of any kind she suffers in savage silence.

    Three days pass before all trace of acrimony
disappears from her responses. I keep up
an indifferent stance, while all the time afraid
that she will leave. It's a little reassuring,
returning from work at dusk, to see a lighted window.
If I lose her now it will mean inner death.

That echoes a few days later
when, alarmed by the shouts and barking,
I run to where she, out walking, has been forced off the road
by a bloody-minded driver who is screaming
that the dogs have scratched his car. I vaguely recognize the man:
he has a weekend cottage about nine miles off, downriver,
and is one of those red-necked yahoos
who bitterly insist on their time-honored right
to litter, to destroy, and to have access to the deviation road
that was laid out a hundred years ago for horse-drawn wagons
to travel to and from the mill, and that runs entirely across our land.
Given this setup, the dogs, seeing a strange car passing through,
or slowing on the bridge, where drivers often linger to take in the view,
feel it's an insufferable invasion of their domain, and at once give chase,
and sometimes, it's true, leap at the sides of cars to emphasize their wrath.
In any case, I tell him to take his claim to the township council,
who should long ago have closed the road, and to Esther,
     who is yelling too,
I say *Please cool it. There's no real damage done.*
At which she flares up, and strides off furiously,
and I, suggesting the guy had better go, hurry after her,
catch up by the barn, and seizing her arm, say:
He's local. We have to try to keep things peaceful around here.
She turns with flaming eyes and tears herself free.

That bastard nearly ran me down!
If you can't even give support— you'll lose me! she cries.
And then walks on, away.

The next morning, a Monday, she suddenly leaves for the city,
driving off with a terse good-bye and set, sullen lips.
Each day, then evening, then night I think she might return,
but tensely the week wears on. I strain for signs of her,
but the road remains empty, the breeze unbroken,
and the house is again muffled and dim.
Then on Friday, when I am downstairs in the kitchen,
opening a tin of sardines for supper,
there comes a startling, clickety tattoo of steps,
and a joyous, hysterical piping from the dogs,
and the door scraping — and she bursts in, her face alight,
and her legs colliding with clumps of bulging shopping bags.
You poor man! she cries. *You must be starved!*
She is wearing a tight black dress, nylons, high heels,
her hair pulled back and held by amber combs —
stunning, all of it, as when I had first seen her,
and for a moment I am too awed to do much more than stare.
Then I quickly go and take the groceries from her,
and venture a darting kiss, at which she laughs

and hugs me hard, and her forms so fill that dress
— she had got it from Helen — that I am ready to drop everything
and push her towards our bed, but she breaks away,
throws off her shoes and runs downstairs calling:
How did you manage? There wasn't anything to eat!
    I know then that whatever I think an occasion calls for,
she will always turn it inside out; and that impulse is part
of her contrariness, of that basic suspicion of established order
that makes her elusive and alluring.

    Her shopping bags seem cornucopias —
she takes from them such an incredible variety of foods,
most in crisp store wrap, but some in homey reused containers,
waxed paper, rumpled foil. Esther! There's her mother's *gefilte fish:*
patties of minced whitefish and pike simmered in an ambrosial broth,
and to spice them, ground horseradish sweetened and reddened by beet,
and a magnificent golden brown egg loaf, thickly braided
      like a maiden's hair,
and bagels, which feel to me still warm!, sprinkled with
      toasted sesame seed,
and half a hearty round gray-brown rye, smelling of savory caraway,
and moist, fleshy slices of smoked carp, glistening paprika red,
and a jar of silvery herring and sliced onions in a creamy marinade,

and a whole white cottage cheese, still shaped as it was by its cotton bag,
and corpulent, wrinkled black olives, slick from their oil and brine,
and several kinds of slinky sausage, the meat dotted with garlic and fat,
and, my God, a whole rosy roasted chicken, its severed knees
provocatively spread — but now I see a kind
     of buckwheat stuffing inside.
And the bags aren't half empty . . . Out comes a container
     of chopped liver,
and one of her mother's delicious mix of carrots, raisins and prunes,
and another of mushrooms and rice. And even a pot of thick pea soup,
and — though we have quarts and quarts of our own — a big jar
of pink applesauce, and a compote of peaches and pears. And more fruit:
bananas and oranges, nectarines, unseasonal cherries
     from who knows where, dates,
and even a few dark dried pods of strange, sweet, Saint-John's-bread.
Then there's a dense, velvety honey cake, crusted with almonds,
and some sugary blueberry buns, and a single chocolate éclair,
and — oddly imperfect — a pale, limp, leaking lemon pie.
    Such abundance overwhelms the kitchen table.
We move to the one in the dining room, which normally seats eight,
and opened, twelve, and it too is soon completely spread.
Then Esther gleefully makes a salad of our own fresh greens —
some late lettuce and parsley I'd brought in, I thought
     for a number of meals —
and while I'm opening a bottle of our chokecherry wine
she heats up the soup and broils potatoes too!
    Esther—I beg *who will eat all this?*

You! she says, and indeed isn't happy, and keeps urging me on,
teasing and tempting, frowning, even bullying a bit,
until I've at least had a taste of each dish.

Overstuffed, I've learnt another important rule about my wife,
perhaps one that sums her up. It's that whatever she feels,
she's unbridled about. With her, emotion is everything,
and in action that becomes everything at once,
everything without stint, in short —
everything to excess.

The next day we're at table, having lunch,
sitting kitty-cornered, close, completely reconciled,
when all at once, solemnly, she says:
There's just one thing I'll ask of you . . .
Inwardly I freeze, wondering if it all has led to this.
Will you do it? she says.
I'd like to point out that I don't know what *it* is,
but, a little frightened, I forego that reasonableness,
and trying to seem tolerant, tamely nod.
I want you to say the blessing for meals.
The blessing! A grace! But I've been a lifelong skeptic,
and she, I know, is an unbeliever to her bones —
the very idea puffs me up with principled rage.

Why? I ask. She smiles shyly, and that shyness undoes me.
I like ritual she says.

She teaches it to me in Hebrew, word for word.
Translated, it goes: *Blessed be the Lord our God,*
King of the universe, who brings forth bread from the earth.
For wine, I learn to say *brings forth the fruit of the vine.*
It's simple enough, once I have it by rote, and decorative,
and seems to call for some fond gesture — a look, a kiss,
        a touch of hands,
that for a moment makes us mindful of each other
before we begin to eat.

We've rented the other house to a professor of Asian art.
He lives alone there, with a cat, using the basement and the top floor
for his books. He has thousands — they line the walls; and his collection
of classical records, including jazz, takes up a whole side
        of the living room.
The long drive to and from his office he makes every working day;
we can't understand why sometimes he returns in between,
when a hour or so later he has to go back to give another class.
He says *It's to breathe the air. I need it for my soul.*
A suave fellow, with a dark moustache upcurled in the grand manner,
subtle, cosmopolitan, he seems, despite his unaccented speech,

slightly foreign — French perhaps, or even from some more exotic strain;
we haven't and we don't think to ask.

On the first Friday he's home we invite him to share a meal with us.
To head him off as he lifts his glass I burst out with the blessing,
and he pauses and looks amused. His eyes flit from the candles
to the braided bread, the waiting wine, the steaming chicken soup.
I feel ill at ease and begin to explain that our blessing, on this night,
heralds the Sabbath joy. *Oh, I know* he says. *I can recite it for you.*
Esther and I both think it's some cultural baggage he's picked up,
like a Moslem prayer or Buddhist chant, but no, he says,

        he learnt it as a child.
He's a Jew, it seems, but so assimilated as to have almost forgotten it.
In any case, he falls in with what we do, and his joining us

        becomes routine,
virtually itself a rite. But his eyes retain their touch of ridicule.

Weeks go by, then one weekend he goes to see his family
in Philadelphia; he has parents, sisters, nephews and nieces there.
On the following Friday we ask him how it was. *Awful!* he exclaims.
Everyone fell on their food! He shakes his head. *I didn't realize
how significant the blessing is.* He stares at us, and then,
somewhat embarrassed, looks away. *For me it's come to separate,* he says
the sacred meal from the profane day.

The professor has grown familiar with Esther;
he takes her arm, touches her shoulder, holds her hand.
Then one evening, on the stairs, while going down to dinner,
and laughing gaily about something said, he playfully
puts his fingers on her back and slides them round her waist.

I wait until she's gone into the kitchen,
and keeping my voice as low and level as I can, say to him:
She's wonderful, I know, but she is, my friend, my wife . . .
His eyes flash with alarm. *Look, but don't touch!* I add,
suddenly giving way to more fury than I knew I felt.
He flushes deeply; and, when he has rallied, is submissively polite.

But later I feel badly for us both. I remember once,
years before Esther, being told by a most generous, gentle host:
You've been, and still are, welcome in my house,
but I'd be pleased if you wouldn't make passes at my wife.
I was mortified! The more so because I realized there was substance
to what he'd said. Weeks earlier I had handed her a little note,
a few romantic lines written out of loneliness and longing

for what she was;
because I did it in his sight I thought he'd understood — and he had:
he had grasped, better than I, that within my mawkish nonchalance
there was an unsettling bid to win his woman.

I left at once and never could go back.

What did you say to him? Esther asks;
for she has, of course, noticed the professor's new restraint.
Though I don't answer, my hesitant silence tells enough.
You should have left him to me she goes on. *I can handle men.*
But how? I wonder. He's much better looking than me,
and nearer her age than mine. Perhaps they have a right...
I know that if I have to depend on our piece of paper,
or deliberately to invoke our bond, I won't have her very long.
But the idea of losing her still stops me cold.
I think I'll go to the city she says.
Again! I cry. It's been only three days since she was last there.
I want to do some work she says. *I might be gone all week.*
Where?
Oh, at the library, probably.
No— where will you stay?
Oh... Maybe at Jim's.
She means it, I can see. Jim is the non-fiction writer
she's doing research for. He's divorced, and has a high-rise suite.
There's an extra room she adds.
I'm shocked and scared, but know I have to be careful, even cunning.
What if he comes in during the night? No, not to force you, I say
but to plead that because he's lonely, or is suffering in some way...
Don't be silly! she says. *He's a child. He's no more crafty than a kitten.*
But you would cuddle a kitten I think. And in a despairing, fateful rush:

It won't look right! Damn it, you're a married woman!
And I'm being choked she exclaims. *I can't breathe!*
You might if you'd try thinking of more than yourself.
I'll kick you! she cries, and then she does. But as her feet are bare —
she often goes barefoot in the house — the blow itself is painless.
Yet she has never struck me before. I say *Don't start that. I'm stronger!*
And her face flinches as if I'd already hit her.
We look distraught into each other's eyes. An instant opens
in which she can be reached, but, unentered, it ominously closes.
Mutely, I feel there's nothing I can bargain with,
that all I have is what I am, and I can't yield on that.

 I won't stay with you! she cries. And she runs and gets her coat and purse,
flings on a scarf, and rushing out, slams both the doors.

 I am suddenly struck with delight! Moving swiftly after her,
scrambling the surprised dogs, I stop on the threshold of the porch.
She's already halfway down the walk, in six inches of fresh snow.
Esther—I call *hadn't you better take your boots?*

 She laughs, laughs hard, then cries.
And we shed a few more tears in the house,
thinking how close a call we've had.
We go to bed to warm her feet. And to hallow
the humbling wonder of our love.

Afterwards, when she is lying by my side, recovering her breath,
I ask her if it has ever been like this with any other man.
Well . . . she says *it always came easily to me, so I seldom got left out,*
but no, never so many times. That's very strange and special.
She squints at me through her lashes. *Once, early on with us,* she says
I tried to keep track, but lost count when we were nearing ten.
By then my mind was melting too. Mostly it's as if I'm music,
soaring up, and up and up, bursting through, then floating down,
        and up again,
over and over. You play my body— it's trite— but truly, like an orchestra.
Well, but not because of any conscious means; I've never seen a sex book
or read a manual. It's because I wait until a mutual feeling begins to flow,
and then follow where it leads. But of course it does take two.
Despite the violent passion Esther brings to arguments, in bed she's loyal
and giving, and becomes a tender, trusting friend.

Months ago, when we were married, we were given
        the usual wedding gifts,
but a last one, the package covered with canceled stamps, came today
from a friend of Esther's who's spending a sabbatical year in Europe.

I unwrapped it: a graceful Italian flower vase glazed in a clear, rich blue.
It had been stuffed with newspapers, and as I pulled them out
my eye was caught by a small picture of a handsome, white-haired head
with a sensitive, somehow familiar face. I smoothed it and carefully read
the caption; it was an obituary, and he, war correspondent, novelist, poet,
had been Esther's last great love before she came to me —
        their flaming affair
had literally taken them across oceans and from desert sands
        to arctic snows.
When she had shown me a snapshot of him I hadn't known
        whether to be jealous
or grateful, because, considerably older than me,
        his age had been my assurance
that mine wouldn't be the problem I had at first imagined it might be.
    She came when I called her, smiling at my having found something
of interest in the stuffing, and leaned over to look at what I pointed to.
Her lips opened, and then closed to contain the pain. She turned away
and walked out, quietly shutting first the front door
        and then the porch's too.
I watched her through a window, and was relieved to see
        that she had put on
her rubber boots; otherwise she was wearing only a sweater and slacks,
but luckily sunlight was now spreading across the snow, and the weather,
in the wake of a cold morning, had turned mild for a midwinter's day.
    About ten minutes later I followed, and saw her standing by the forest,
beyond the trampled track, where the sun, already slipping
        behind the hills,

94

was just then giving way to shade. The dogs ran on ahead, but I could see,
from the way her back was bent, that she was locked in grief,
        and they too,
when they reached her, sensed that and were still. I put her coat
around her shoulders, pressed them gently, and retraced my steps.
It was early, but at the stable I went in and did the chores;
for I didn't want her to be alone when she came home.
    I knew she was in mourning not only for him, but that his death
had opened the caverns of all the dead who dwelt in her,
        so many of them,
from those she could still put a lively image to, to the large
        extended family
whose ashes had disappeared into the dirt around the Nazi death camps.
And she had been born in a camp, one to which her parents,
        scarcely alive,
their starved arms scarred by tattooed numbers, had after the liberation
been taken to be restored to health, and where they had met, and married,
and miraculously, it seemed then — made her. I'm just beginning
to comprehend the dark immensity of horror, doom and rage
that underlies her vivacious, splendid surface.

    She was a long time coming back to life.
She made meals, milked the goats, got me to fix the dog door —

a small push-pull one that lets them use the porch at will,
but only outwardly was she with the rest of us. Happily, though,
for a time there was no more talk of going to the city;
as it is, her work there adds nothing to our meager funds —
the little she earns is more than canceled out by the cost of gas,
the cleaner's bills and café snacks, and the extravagant gifts she gives
to whomever she stays with; really, we subsidize her free lancing
to satisfy her restlessness.
    She did, however, start riding almost daily
on her palomino mare — hers by her and the horse's mutual choice —
and her long hair and the mare's blonde mane would both bounce
as the animal bounded up the snow-covered slopes, to vanish with her
for hours at a time, until cold or darkness drove them down.
Once I went too, but my gelding hung back behind the mare's tail,
unwilling to challenge her dominance, or even to break the trail,
and when in front they went into a gallop I deliberately
      held him back,
reluctant to risk my neck and his on the hidden ice slicks underfoot.
While ahead they waited disdainfully for us to catch up.
    My wife not only rides well, she swims strongly,
dances superbly, skis, plays tennis and can sail a boat —
skills she learnt from lovers and now largely wasted in her life with me.
Such furious activity, and her hair-trigger temper, her laughter,
her bursts of affection, her moods of mute joy and numbing grief
are, I realize, the intense, magnified acting out of what she feels,
and I know her need to be touched, and held, and her hunger for love,
and the hop-skip way her mind works to arrive at arresting thoughts,

and that she's often afraid; yes, all that I understand, and yet
there are rhythms in her I just don't recognize.

Her skin always astonishes me.
It's so incredibly smooth and soft, moist and warm,
not only on her face and neck, but also on her shoulders and back,
arms and sides, breasts and belly, thighs and calves,
and between her legs; her soles alone are hard, from going barefoot.
Every bit of her is wonderfully enclosed in that supple,
faintly lustrous skin, which is like a life-giving fountain
flowing endlessly over her.

Esther unnerves me. I've hewn the forest,
and survived in a sleeping bag the rigors of winter,
and built with my own hands and sinews several shelters,
and conducted my affairs so that I have a manageable debt,
and I can now, with a sense of my strength as a man and a person,
stand confidently in my domain, seeing the pleasant order and plenty
I've brought here, and how it charms and soothes the spirit of others,

and I can calmly meet anyone's gaze and unflinchingly answer for my acts.
But she, with a single angry word, which tears like a jagged knife,
or a sudden jolting smile that's a lightning flash of love,
instantly undercuts my inner stance, making me crumble in despair
or melt in delight, and reduces me to a crazed and hurting
or an intoxicated child. It bewilders me that I can withstand all the world
but never, not even for a moment, her.

Plain as I am, women have loved me,
women — like my wife — who could virtually choose whom they wished,
and I've had to ask myself why. It's not because of what
        I've done for them —
that's been so little; the balance has been all the other way.
Nor was it for my charm — I have a horror
        of being taken for what I'm not.
I think, rather, it's because of the love of women
        I've had from childhood on,
and an attitude of tender realism mingled with exalting awe.
I'm simply moved by the pain and stress of being female,
of having always to look good, of needing to nurture and to care,
and I'm deeply moved by the miracle of giving life, and such sweet milk,
and by womanly good humor in the face of threatened terror,
and by the age-old rage smouldering beneath those vulnerable breasts.

Perhaps all these feelings are in my eyes when I look at a woman,
and when she notices, they sometimes speak to her.

To me there's something sanctified about food and women,
and I never approach one or the other with dirty hands.
Even in the woods, if I'm to eat, I must first find a spring or pool
in which to wash; otherwise the food will choke me going down.
And in the same way the parts I make love with must be always clean.
Yet most men — almost all I've seen — wash their hands after they pee,
presumably because they've handled something dirty, or at least
not nice; I do the opposite — for that's my purest part,
and to sully it would be to rob from what I most respect.
Normally I say nothing about this, nor ever make of it a ritual or show,
but when women come into my arms they somehow sense
the deep regard it represents, and are both stirred and comforted.
In the male world obsessed by sex I wonder why it isn't better known
that women are most turned on by tenderness.

You don't love me, Esther says suddenly today,
as we are mucking out the stable *you love only the idea of me.*
And the twinge of truth that causes leaves me for a moment dumb.
Then I say *No*—*I **also** love the idea of you.*
Too late! she cries. *You had to think about it!*
And her lips go on smiling, but their corners crease
       into a hint of hurt.

She gradually becomes sad and silent,
distant, uninvolved. I desperately want her close again,
and when I am showering, ahead of her — she likes
the lingering smell of manure, she comes into the bathroom
      for something
and I suggest that she join me. *It will save water* I say.
She hesitates, and then as if swayed by that strips off her clothes
and with a chill *Nothing personal*. . . lifts the curtain and steps in.
Such sudden beauty! I widen my eyes, which only makes her shrug,
and though she tries to treat my glances as a flirting game,
her presence really is cool, her skin taut under the gaily-splashing spray.
But she accepts my nearness, and soon lets me soap her back,

and then her breasts, and then turn her round and kiss her mouth,
and in my ardent embrace under the hot water she begins to melt,
and we couple first standing up, and then awkwardly lying in the tub,
where under the streaming shower, which blessedly stays hot
— I'm so glad now she'd talked me into the larger,
        more expensive tank! —
I keep at her, repeatedly, trying to squeeze affection from her flesh,
until she pleads, palms up, that she's both sore and spent.
It has been a rape, which did no good; for as I lie against
her softened skin there escapes from it the tremor of a troubled sigh,
and I feel guilty, defeated, and then deeply ashamed.

The explosion I expect doesn't come.
Instead her growing despair is soon edged with grief,
which imperceptibly changes to rage, and her responses,
when they come, are abrupt, hostile, and frighteningly terse.
Moreover, she's surprisingly efficient — cooking just enough,
tidying our books, even sorting out for me the bills to pay.
Gone is the exuberant extravagance I'd often complained of,
and am now sorry, extremely sorry, to lose.

When she leaves I'm standing by a window
and watch her go. She looks sleek, in her black twill cap
and short sheepskin jacket, and the tight dark skirt
that stops abruptly above the high-heeled city boots,
leaving her knees, like her face, ambiguously bare.
    All night I'd lain sleepless by her side,
kept by hurt and fear from touching that warm skin
that had always before sought mine. And after a day of silence
I had come in from chores to find her packed, and bathed,
and pinning up her hair, and her fragrance everywhere.
    I can smell it still, faintly, and it makes me feel
my failure all the more. I had loved her looks, her verve,
her social skills, but never the complex, intense whole of her;
that I had only observed. And even now I am stubbornly looking on,
after letting her walk out without a word.
    She's quit the path, made icy by the strong March sun,
which has also set free eager shoots against the house,
and supporting her suitcase with her thigh is gamely staggering on,
followed by the affable, ever-approving, tail-wagging dogs,
interestedly sniffing her spike holes in the snow.
    At the garage she backs out the old
dependable jeep — her own car is laid up, waiting for a part,
and then she pats the dogs, speaks — lovingly, it seems — to each,
and looking straight ahead drives slowly across the bridge,

where suddenly she smiles — and still smiling, speeds away!

It's a stab, that smile, that joy — it makes me gasp.
It instantly undoes what we are — even quells my feeling for her flesh.
I hate her for spurning us, for scorning all I've felt.
I cry for a fatal auto crash — then conversely *No, God, no!*
Don't interfere— oh Jesus, please! Please let her be.

Calming down, I reflect that no one else
could have provoked such murderous violence in me.
But what does she want? I've been faithful, attentive, adoring,
I've labored to the limit of my energy; and except for just a few,
our nights have all been sweet. No it goes beyond all that.

She wants to be loved just as she is,
completely — with all of her mercurial impulses.
The trouble is, I've seen too much to be that blind again.
And I too want acceptance as I am, with all my qualms and faults.
I'd hoped, I guess, for some fond pity as well as passion.

Later, resigned, turning out the lights behind me
as I go up to bed, I pause to gaze at the forbidding night,
and, to my surprise, think I see a tiny intermittent glow
coming from the dark mass of the distant other house. *Strange,* I think
the professor isn't due back for another week.

Esther has been watering his plants while he's away;
the key is under his front mat. *Maybe I'd better check* I think.
And out I go, feeling it's probably a fool's errand, and shivering;
for with darkness has come frost and a sharp damp wind
that is driving flurries of small stinging flakes.

Across the bridge, going up the hillside steps

to the professor's terrace, I begin, untypically, to feel afraid,
and wish I'd brought my gun. *That's crazy* I think, and then see —
the jeep! Already snow covered, it stands bleak and silent on the drive.
Where's Esther? I cry, and move swiftly to the house.

    The tall glass panel is undraped,
and I can see, through the open doorway of the bedroom —
the one whose window faces my place — the pale fitful light
flashing in colors near the bed. *No!* I scream. *Not a brutal assault!*
And I rush raging, blood-blinded, to the door.

    It flies open. I know the twisting hall
and pound to the room, throwing on my flashlight beam —
and there, shocked, lies Esther on the bed, alone. The TV, shining on,
now finishes its silent billboards and bursts into a barrage of sound.
I switch on a lamp. Esther, open mouthed, begins to laugh.

    She turns off the set. Shakily, she smiling,
I frowning from disconcertment and relief, we regard each other warily.
No one would pick me up! she cries, laughing again. Then pouting:
I've never been so humiliated. I got frozen standing there!
I say *But you had the jeep. Why didn't you just drive?*

    She had parked it near the highway, knowing
I would be told of it. *I couldn't leave you without a car* she says.
And I think: *I couldn't have refused to let you take it.*
So even then we'd been an entity, with unspoken rules
and self-enforced, inherent obligations.

    I say *From a neighbor's, you could have called a cab—*
She shakes her head: *And spread the story! Anyway, I was sure the next one,
or the next . . .* She'd held out her thumb, even a leg; the farmers

must have thought her mad or joking, there on the twilit snowy shoulder.
Why did no one stop? she says. *Am I losing my looks?*
She looks beautiful, with her careful grooming spoilt
from sprawling on the bed. Some wisps of hair are hanging down
      her cheek;
I move to brush them back. *That's not enough* she says. *I'm still cold . . .*
and holds out an arm to me. We lie together; then, of course, make love.
Later we have to sponge the damp spot on the spread.
    Back in our own house we eat a late, hot meal,
and go to bed. We're close again — another crisis passed. I say:
Would you have still left in the morning, if you'd been there all night?
She says *No . . .* And I am glad. Yet now I can't forget that for a moment
I had hated her enough to want her dead.

    I awake to a crocus on the pillow,
looming golden where Esther's curving eyelashes should have been.
It's just her kind of impromptu, hazardous gesture —
had I shifted I might have crushed the pretty blossom with my cheek.
Thanks, I say *but look, it's left a yellow pollen stain.*
That's pure sunshine, darling Esther says, and lightly kissing me
she strips the case and flies it from the clothesline,
half seriously proclaiming it our flag of love.

Let's have a picnic! she cries. *A brunch!*
Outside? I say. But actually the sun is bright,
and only traces remain of last night's snow.
Come on, she says *we'll feed the animals first,*
and then I want to concentrate on you.

  We take our horses, with a groundsheet
and a thick sleeping bag rolled behind the saddles,
and on the pommel of mine I carry a wicker hamper,
and hanging from the horn of hers Esther has a string bag
with a big thermos of coffee and a bottle of wine.

  When we've ridden up the south-facing hill
we see large patches of bare leaves and grass,
as if spring has hurried to meet us here,
and the horses spontaneously begin to canter,
and Esther, moving ahead, flings me a happy smile.

  Wait! I shout, and drawing alongside
I reach for her hand and hold it as we ride;
she grins shyly, with such childlike defenselessness
that I'm overwhelmed, and feel an inner leap,
and rashly, there and then, fall in love again.

Lying near the ridge we can see across the valley,
to where it rises above the forest and becomes rolling fields.
Overhead the sky is blue beyond branches of lacy pine,
our horses are quietly nosing and nibbling in the rustling grass,
and off to the side an insect buzzes, flies on, and doubles back.
I kiss my bride and stroke her shoulder and cheek.
Her head is pillowed on her jacket; I slide my fingers to her breasts,
undo the front-fastened brassiere, then the final buttons of her blouse.
  You won't be cold? I say.
Oh no! I'm too warm. And she whispers: *I'd like it, please.*
  I unfasten what is left and she shakes herself loose
and lies there, amid her clothes, in our dry sheltered spot,
surrounded by wide drifts of moist and melting snow.
She is I think *too lovely to touch, like food too nice to eat.*
But she reaches for my shirt and tugs at it,
and I undress and take her, reverently, into my arms.
When we are joined we lie still for a long while in the sun.
And I feel that this might be the ultimate experience,
this feeling of being one, of rooting into the earth,
of being part of the whole pulsating universe.

One day soon after I see Esther by the water,
on her knees, combing out her long wet hair.
She's washed it in the shower, and is letting the breeze
gently blow it dry. The air is summery, the river high from runoff,
and the burgeoning grass is hourly turning a deeper green.
It's so exciting she calls. I nod and smile at her;
she thinks I'm being patronizing and looks away.
But then she turns and squints, and having forgiven me, grins,
and I — marveling at how little it takes for misunderstanding,
feel that our love is like an uncertain flame
floating, more often tossing, on a murky sea.
Essentially I don't know her, and doubt that I ever will.
Yet nothing moves me like her lithe appearance,
her lovely limbs, her laugh and gestures, the subtle perfume
        of her skin.

Each of her breasts
flows out to a sublime fullness
that swells up prowlike from her chest.
They are sloping domes of the most exquisite flesh,

culminating in potent circles of a sweet blushing pink
from which the warm nubbly nipples erect firmly,
succulently, at my slightest touch. Such ambrosial teats:
all my feeling, all my being, becomes centered in my mouth.
Oh my sister, I rejoice in your breasts, I adore them,
I sometimes think I could die between them. Eyes, hands,
lips and tongue just can't pay sufficient homage to them,
and I have to invent new ways of worship, which, you say,
delight and excite you even more. Your breasts, my love,
are a feast. And then there's all the rest of you.

I think I'll make a seder, she says suddenly
for a few friends. I'm surprised and not, in the sense
that nothing is completely unexpected anymore. But I wonder
why her ardor has abruptly taken such a tribal turn.
Oh, it'll mark our new start she says.
    The word *seder* means order, and refers to the succession of readings
and foods that make up the annual Passover ritual meal.
The *seder* tells the story of the biblical exodus from Egypt,
and celebrates survival, freedom, enduring hope, and for some, faith.
It'll be fun! she adds, though it will be for her a first.
Inherently, the *seder* becomes a gathering of family and friends,
and, with all the cleaning, cooking and baking, a crushing burden

for the woman who must prepare it all. Most guests have seen
good wives so tired when they served that they could scarcely stand.
Never mind she says. Then, on the phone, brightly: *Miriam?*

Miriam is coming, with her children, and Sheila of course, and Helen,
maybe with her latest lover. And the couple at whose house we met.
And even Jim, with — to make a point — his new lady friend.
And relatives, and — Esther's geniality grows with her expanding list.
Hey— she says excitedly *we should ask some neighbors too!*
And I, pressed to this, phone the farmers we are friendliest with.
It's like Christmas dinner I tell them; or to those who are pious
I say *You know, it was Christ's last supper . . .* and their voices take on
a suitably reverential tone. And everyone accepts.

Jesus! Esther says, counting names. *We've got thirty-six!*
We begin to hope that some won't come, because where will we
put them all? But we remember tabletops in the barn, buried
behind bales of straw, and also a few folding cots, and sleeping bags.

And I say *we've got a freezer full of food.*
The wrong kind! she cries. *I'm going to do this right.*
Her eyes flash; there's an edge to her voice. Nerves, I guess.
Jitters over the size of what she's taken on. I decide to do
just what she wants. So I build table legs, and benches to make up for
missing chairs. In the end I have a rough U tightly seating thirty.
Okay she says crossly. *Six can sit on the stairs!*
Esther, I say *knock it off. There's no more room. It's only
a party.* She looks at me like I'm crazy. *Don't you understand
that it's our only way of paying back all we've had from them?
Get me money to give gifts and I'll drop the whole damn thing!*

Don't talk nonsense I say.

She knows there's no money and now no way out of going on with it.

I can't believe she'd bring on the shame that canceling it would cause.

I silently cover the tables with white cloths and they don't look too bad.

Flowers would help, and I suggest gathering violets and marsh marigolds.

No she says. *Sheila is bringing bouquets.*

She's immersed in her cooking; big pans and pots are bubbling

on the stove. Her face is averted, drawn, showing the effects

of several three-or-four-hour nights. Today I found her napping

in the afternoon, but even asleep she seemed intent, anxious, ill at ease.

Why don't you quit early I say. *You'll need your strength tomorrow.*

Why can't you leave me alone! she shouts. Then adds: *I'll be all right.*

That night I try to make love, thinking it might relax us both.

She submits, at first unresponsively. But bit by bit rhythms are roused

and she softly explodes a number of times. Then she sleeps; I don't.

Get some blocks! she says. *Quickly— before they come.*

At the last minute she's decided we have to raise a table

that's an inch lower than the rest. Perhaps because I haven't slept

her impatience irritates me; all day it's been do this, fetch that,

don't talk — she's been isolated and armored by all she has to think about.

Hi! Miriam calls, opening the door. Her kids race down the stairs.

Hey! I say. *Watch the tables—* and barely save some of the settings.

Esther, crying *Oh my God, look how you've grown!* seizes the children

and whirls them about, forcing me back against the center post.

She remembers only when she's finished fussing with them.

Okay, she says *you meet the guests while I shower and get dressed.*

I haven't showered either, or had time to shave, and it makes me

III

acutely uncomfortable. It's crucial, I concede, that she look and feel good,
but being continually submissive is belittling, and I resent it
more than I would care to show. *But,* I think *we'll kiss and make up.*
     Trying to do that, I say *You look great!* when she emerges
          damp and rushed.
Here, she says, holding me off with a pillow *put this on your chair.*
What for? I say, though I know it's because "this night we eat leaning",
Roman style, to show that we are free. But I'm stung by her rejecting me,
and say *Put it on your own chair. I won't be ready in time.*
We'll wait she says. *Just hurry up. You have to conduct.*
Yes ma'am! Pull harder I say. It's unkind, but I have a sudden sense
of being a puppet pulled by strings. *Strings of love* I add with scorn.
She sort of understands. *We'll discuss that later* she says. *Now get going!*
There are already a dozen people downstairs. More are coming
          up the walk.
I don't think so I whisper. *I've had it with your orders.*
Damn you— she cries *if you can't cooperate, I don't need you!*
Fine! I say. I can see the rational arguments — she's high-strung,
harrowed, not herself, and for a second I feel a sad tenderness for her,
but against that rises all the times she's turned on and off.
Good-bye I say, and quietly go out.
The people now arriving are more her friends than mine, so I nod to them
and amble to the road, where there's a long line of parked cars.
In a muddled way I feel what I've done is monstrous,
          that I should go back,
but pride pushes me on, past the barn and the professor's house,
          up the hill.

It's all yours, your majesty I mutter. Then: *I'm sorry . . .*

Looking down in the half dark I can see the professor's outside light,
and him making his way down the steps to join the *seder.*

Maybe he'll preside;
he or any man can: Esther, who knows the ceremony, will prompt him.
I'm being foolish; this is pointless, and yet, I feel, ominously profound.
Yoo-hoo— where are you? Miriam's voice comes from beyond the barn.
Damn her I think. But I know she won't stop. *Up here* I call,
and she swings
the beam of her flashlight back and forth across the hill. Then I hear her
trudging up the road, crunching gravel underfoot. *Where?* she calls.
I get up for a moment. She comes on cautiously
and joins me on my rock.
Do you know what you're doing to her? she says.
She'll manage I reply. Miriam sighs, shifting her heavy bosom.
It's tearing her apart she says. Then when I am silent: *Whatever caused it,
you can put it aside for now. Think of how she feels, with all those people.*
It's never how I feel, I notice. *Be a sport* she says. *Unbend. Come down.*
I can't I say. *I'm not shaved or washed or dressed.*
Gate crash! she says, and giggles. Then she stands to go. *Can I tell her
you're coming?* With that everything gathers, and balances, trembling.
The now-trivial issues recede. Basically, it's Esther's will or mine.
I'm forced to choose between my sense of self and the bride I madly loved.
No . . . Sheer panic. But: *Let it be.* My heart is pounding all of me.
Miriam's indignant glare I can feel through the chill. *All right* she says,
and tramps away, to close ranks. I gaze at our house. It's all alight,
while I'm here in the dark, left out, looking on, and again, alone.

113

It's icy cold. The straw stabs,
and tastes of dust. Pinpricks of low stars
glitter between the barn boards. Mice scratch;
below, a horse stirs in the stable.
The sharp stench of manure mingles with
the dry smell of overwintered hay.
Now, looking inward or out, my eyes
see only black upon black.

The last overnight guest is going to his car
when I approach; I suppose whoever came with him
left with others, while he stayed and flirted with my wife.
I scarcely know him, and am glad he pretends not to see me;
then he feigns surprise and nods as he drives by.
With all of them gone the place seems to revive, draw breath;
the dogs too, who came dolefully nosing me in the barn at night,
are now dancing, wheeling with joy as I push past them to the porch.
The living room is a shambles: sheets and sleeping bags and towels
lie tangled; Esther must have insisted that no one tidy up.
Hello? I say. A hush. Then I hear, listlessly: *Oh, the man of action . . .*

She's lying on our bed, eyes almost shut, obviously exhausted.
She squints with sad rancor as I stand in the doorway, staring.
I'm not leaving she says. *I won't give you the satisfaction.*

Crazily, it's the rhyme, intended or not, that gives me hope;
it's a crack in her cold harsh wall of ridicule and reproach.
I sit beside her on the bed. Her look stays fixed, defiant.
I'm not going anywhere she says again. *You're stuck with me.*
And I won't ever forgive you, or forget. I say nothing.
My gaze goes from her face to her soft throat, her rounded shoulder,
the snug, V-necked sweater swollen by her breasts. I can see
a bit of their sweated crease; and affected, as always, by her flesh,
on impulse I slowly move a tentative finger towards it.
Her arm comes up to knock my hand away, then stops, and settles back.
And her eyes spitefully glint when I meet taut, unyielding skin.
I sit awhile in silence, absorbing all the implications.
She remains mute, unmoving. But when I go she calls out:
Don't touch anything. I'll do it. I don't want help from you!

In the dining room tables have been pushed back,
chairs and benches overturned, sugar, crumbs and napkins scattered.
The kitchen is cluttered with uneven stacks of dirty dishes,
piles of platters, roasting pans, dozens of glasses with dregs of wine.
A heap of greasy cutlery is soaking in the sink; while on the stove,
congealed, are breakfast remnants of *matzos* and eggs. A disorder
as complete as between Esther and me. But a bit easier to put right.
I roll up my sleeves and wash dishes, stack after stack, not stopping
until the counters and table are clear. Tired then, hungrily
I eat some leftovers of last night's feast. The food makes me drowsy:
it's been two nights since I've had any sleep. Going upstairs,
I hear a strange, sibilant, rhythmic rasp — it's my wife, deep asleep,
and lightly snoring. She seems disarmed, wide open now. I'd like
to embrace her, but I leave between us a scrupulous space.

She's gone when I next open my eyes.
I can hear her below, shifting chairs and banging on the tables.
When I go down I see she has straightened the living room,
and has finished washing up: a mountain of pans and odds and ends
stand drying on the drainboard. More optimistic now, I quietly join

in taking apart the tables, and as I move them out she sweeps the floor.
We don't speak except for working words, but I think willy-nilly
we share a sense of wiping things clean, as if the whirlwind has passed
and we, in a way and actually, are picking up the pieces.
Indeed, later, she casually calls me to sit down for supper.
But when I catch her hand to draw her to me for a kiss —
long our established prelude — she fiercely pulls back, her eyes flashing
a warning; and then she stifles a sob, forcing me to feel
that I've robbed the ritual of what it once had meant.

I am already in bed when she undresses,
and then stops by the bureau to file down a nicked fingernail.
Nudity never embarrasses her — she knows her forms will please,
but I can't help irritably thinking that tonight's display
underlines my disentitlement, and her tart, adamant disdain.
I should turn away; but in the low light of the bedside lamp
she looks utterly beautiful. From her bent head her hair is spilling,
curling onto her small, curved shoulders, which flow into slender arms
tapering to graceful fingers, and her body — an elongated figure eight,
larger in the lower round, with those perfect joys above
       and that alluring
crease below — is supported on such shapely, smooth and sturdy legs.
It's the totality of her nakedness — of late she hasn't even worn

her wedding ring, saying it rubs her skin — that I find unnerving:
it hides so well the festering hurt within.

We've never worn clothes of any kind in bed,
except for the first night she came here,
when we had talked so long it was too late for her to drive back,
and I quickly warmed the spare bedroom I'd frugally kept closed,
but that May had been cool, and the thickly-filled mattress stayed cold,
so she was shivering when I told her to come in with me,
and I saw she had on a thin gown her handbag must have held.
We didn't touch then, but our carnal tension caused such torment
that even the next night, after loving, we still ached from it.
And now we lie here, side by side, with skins long used to touching,
and their magnetism is marred, spoilt, by all our inner turmoil.
At last I say *This is stupid. Stuff it! I'll sleep on the couch.*
No, she cries *I will!* And springing up she stumbles over some folds
and falls against me hard, hitting her head on mine. *Hey . . .* I say.

I'm holding her, my mouth to her ear. *You okay?* I say.
Yes she sighs. *Let go.* I keep hold. *Come on,* she says *don't be cute.*
I tell her she just can't make an exit. *Unlike you!* she snaps.
Well, you pushed me to it I say. *You were so damn despotic.*
Oh, was I? And your precious dignity couldn't take it, eh?
Don't needle I say. *I'm sick of being your stooge, your yoyo.*
You dope! she cries. *You puffed-up, self-absorbed, rigid, fragile fool—*
you'd go to pieces if I didn't keep you flattered and fucked!
Why not fed too? I say, galled. This woman is alien, grotesque.
But you're right I say, releasing her. *Don't put up with me. Go.*
No she says. *I'm past that now. I've invested too much in you.*
That's the trouble I think. We want love and then are trapped by it.
We both sit for a while, silently suffering aftershock.
Then I heave a heavy sigh, and she quietly begins to cry.

Her tears please me; then at once I'm rueful, sad and tender,
and I want, need, hunger to hug her — to kiss her eyes, nose, cheeks,
to fasten on her moist mouth and feel the common current flow.
She pushes me away at first, but I persist, and slowly
she yields, and lets me whisper loving words, and stroke the right spots,

and I sense her juices rising . . . her body becoming free.
But when she's aroused she suddenly says *Ah, why? It won't work.*
It will! I say. *It's a way to survive.* She thinks about that,
then says *All right. Give me a minute.* And goes to the bathroom.
I wait, randy. She washes, comes back, rather coolly lies down
and lets me make repeated, ardent, violent love to her.
And responds: her passion even reaches wild and sobbing surges.
But something has changed. Despite trying, I can't really move her.
I've been shut out from her core, and might never again get in.

   The thrill of seeing the river and pond each morning
is missing today; nor am I stirred by the first ferns.
With ill will I hear, in faint waves from far in the woods,
the rasping whine of a chain saw: someone's stealing there.
I should investigate, but I don't feel like going.
Damn, I wish the dogs would, but if I order them to
they'll only look puzzled, then doubtfully wag their tails.
There are trees I should cut, but now I'm sick of killing;
I'd like to pause, I'd like to mourn what is already dead.

When I go to the spot a few days later
— in a corner of our property, close to a road —
I see that only the portable tops have been taken;
the bugger felled three big healthy maples for firewood
and left the trunks, too much for him, lying in his mud.
He also left beer bottles, cigarette butts, torn bags
and lots of other litter. I feel rage, hate, disgust.

Earlier I said "spot". Once, a visiting crony,
when asked by a rude lady looking for a house lot
if there were any nice spots she could see, answered her:
Madam, alas, this property is not a leopard.
And it's not. Not for crass perversion or for pillage —
this forest is a living affirmation of life.
But even if I patrolled it with a machine gun,
posted signs, called in the police, I couldn't prevent
the mean-spirited, savage vanity of people
who delight in deliberately — there's no need now —
destroying growing plants, killing defenseless creatures,
and clogging this natural garden with their garbage.

What evil mix is it of religious rhetoric,
humiliated sex and hostile desperation
that breeds the beast who gets satisfaction from smashing
beer bottles on the rocks of the river? I wonder.
I wonder at such malevolence, and at my own.

It begins to rain when I'm cutting the maple logs
— I came back with the tractor, and will use the loader
to move the heavy chunks to the trailer by the road —
and shutting off the noisy saw I pause to look up
at the three holes torn in the lacy dome of branches,
and I think about what's coming down in those big drops:
sulfuric acids, nitric acids, other toxins
that ruin leaves, bark, stems, seep into the ground, enter roots
and slowly kill — trees, lakes, streams, the water food chain, fish.
Elsewhere they kill more rapidly, I read. Already
whole maple forests have been poisoned in the east.
Here our limestone soil seems to have acted, for a time,
as an antidote; death has been just a bit delayed.

When I get home she has the table nicely set for supper,
and, smiling, is spiritedly talking on the kitchen phone;
she seems to be making a date, or promising something.
Who was that? I say, and she names a potter, a bachelor
who's been around here a few times, and is hot for her, I've heard.
He lives in a nearby village, where they'll soon be holding
a community crafts show, at which he wants to sell his wares,
and she, knowing I won't go, has said she'll help him. *Why?* I say.
Because I need to learn— I'm learning not to need you she says.
I'm both angered and flattered: I didn't know she did.
But I forego that, and speak instead of the chemical rain.
And, as I guessed, she soon grows slightly anxious: *It'll affect us?*
Sure will I say. *In time, it'll slowly sicken everything.*
And in her burdened silence she comes a little closer.

I don't know what to do about the potter;
she's been seeing more of him than I would like. Since the craft show
they've been twice to movies, and are out now for a twilight walk —
I can see their dark figures swimming against the sunset sky
as they head up the hill, behind the darting, foraging dogs —

and then she'll bring him back for tea, and they'll talk and joke
      for hours.
Truth is, I don't dislike him; he's a bright, easygoing guy,
a refugee from some city rat race, who's educated,
and has a teaching degree that allows him to do supply
whenever he's hard up, and his pottery, though it isn't art,
is honestly and strongly made in a kind of countrified style.
And Esther, aside from what she deems her need, will always find
some men heart-stirring, and will in some way want to be with them,
and I accept her right to be human as well as married.

    But I don't at all like lying in bed, trying to read,
and listening to them laughing down below. So when he leaves
I tell her that feelings are one thing, behavior another.
Really? she says. *I can like him but not see him— is that it?*
It's a matter of degree I say. *Try to keep things balanced.*
What? she cries. *Your prudishness and my pleasure? Well, sir* she adds,
because I seem to dismiss her — *for me it's bare survival.*
And in her hurt eyes I see there's more to this than I had thought.
Look, she says *I love you, and I'll stay, and yes, be faithful too,*
but I can't live up to your rigid idea of our contract
that I should always look good, be sweet, work hard, at your level—
with no chance of achieving it. Your disapproval is for me

as acid as that rain, and I'll wither like those leaves.
I'm horrified to hear her, and pained, but most of all, ashamed.

My bride, you're familiar and fascinating, but who are you?
There are layers and layers of you I don't yet know or love.
What made me believe you were even partly as I saw you —
a vivid, beautiful, intelligent compliment to me,
satisfying my senses and a smug pride of possession,
while in fact, which is funny, my fitful, feeble hold on you
hung on nothing more than a look, a touch, a smile — your feeling
that you wanted to be close to me; and when I've filled you
and you've murmured *So good, so good*... and it seemed final, truly,
we were tied, and tested, only for those moments. You're not mine —
damn, I knew that, but in not wanting to deal with all you are
I turned away from you, and tried depending on formulas.
But if I now try to show you my love is deeper, Esther,
will you ever really be sure it isn't merely gesture?

Jim has stopped in unexpectedly with Beautiful Betty,
the girl he had brought to the *seder*, whom I hadn't met then.
She's hardly even pretty, but all her features are polished
to perfection: clipped, creamed, combed, painted, glued and propped up,
and the whole effect is glamorous — hence the satirical name
the sisterhood has given her. I find her frank and funny;
she laughs freely and good-naturedly about her false nails, bleached hair,
blue contact lenses, uplift bra, and — because she shuns the pill —
her *designer diaphragm*, and though she's had lots of lovers
she hasn't put her faith in any of them, but has worked hard
and saved and bought herself a little house. *I'm just fine* she says.
They're trying to book a resort room for two days, but won't hear
of staying here, though we beg them to; I think Jim's brought her by
to show me, again, that there's nothing between him and Esther.

She's laughing uproariously as I come in the house —
clutching the phone, clenching her hand, then pulling at her hair in glee;
between giggles she mouths *Thomas* — my gentle neighbor to the east,
the one whose calf died the stormy day that I drove over there.
He has a simplistic, childlike humor that charms by its innocence —

for example, when, straight-faced, he holds out his teacup for a refill
his hand shakes, rattling the china in perfect imitation
of Parkinson's, or if you tell him you baked these cookies from scratch,
he'll say gullibly *Not flour. . . ?* then gradually let his eyes smile,
or he'll mail us farm news clippings with his own funny comments.
His affection is seldom physical, except with his pigs and calves,
whose sides and backs he'll scratch because, as he says: *Well . . . they like it,*
but his warmth and good will, and patience, are almost palpable.
Everyone, out of respect, instinctively calls him *Thomas* —
never Tom nor any nickname, and he's been called that all his life;
all who know him somehow sense they're dealing with a saintly soul.

    Esther has become special to him, his pal, his confidante —
he won't even tell his wife some of the strong things he whispers to her.
Sometimes he and Esther will be hours in his stable,
        huddled in smiling talk;
sometimes, especially Sundays after church, he'll come and sit
in our kitchen and chat with her over several cupfuls of tea.
I'm always glad, honored, to see him, but I soon leave them alone;
I've come to recognize that he's now much more her friend than mine.
And I'm frankly pleased for his sake, because he's such a prince
        among men
it sets him apart, leaving few people he can freely be close to.

    Wait! Esther cries. *Give me that line again—* and she grabs a pen:
it seems it's a childishly pornographic poem that Thomas
is reciting to her, one for which he got punished in grade school
when he didn't realize the double, gross meaning of it.
At times I wonder whether his wife minds his keen friendship with Esther;

she seems to treat it as a fated phenomenon of his nature,
as wild, as inevitable in its way, as the weather.

A flat, heavy rain has been falling for hours,
after drizzle and showers for almost six days.
The sodden earth, already drowned, can't hold much more;
sustained rivulets are coursing down the slopes,
feeding the roaring, swollen, muddy river
that's carrying part of our topsoil to the sea.
This disaster is totally indifferent
to me: to what I profess, or think, or feel.

I have a sinking feeling about this spring,
as if my last choices are fast slipping away.
I thought I was free, in both love and my life here,
but I'm being forced to face reality.
My wife wants a commitment to what she is,
and the land too needs much more than I'm giving it.

And to evade the challenge of either of those
means inwardly to give up, decline — and die.

    The horses are now daily let out to roam,
while the goats, their stable door wide open, go in and out at will.
Though there's not yet enough grass for much grazing,
        both come grudgingly
to the hay I take out to them; they're tired of it after eating all winter
the equivalent of dry breakfast food and water,
and a little grain occasionally sweetened by molasses.
Being out feels much better to them, and the sun's warmth stimulates.
But I see that by midday the horses are heading towards shade,
and most of the goats have gone back in. The sun isn't as benign
as it was; its heat feels harsher now, and I notice I get burnt
sooner than before. I suppose it's because we've thinned the ozone,
formerly our faithful sunshade in the sky.
    Going home, I see Esther sitting on the stone steps
that sweepingly curve down to the kitchen at the back of the house.
She's reading; she hasn't really wanted to join me at chores
since our big blowup over the *seder*, and I haven't pushed her.
Now I want to tell her to wear a sun hat, but my steps are soft
as I approach, and she doesn't see me. I stop, and spellbound, stare.

The slight bend and turn away of her head and neck, the graceful line
of her temple, with stray hairs swaying, and of her smooth cheek and chin,
and the tip of her nose, all seem to me touchingly beautiful,
the symbol, even the embodiment of all I most care for.
It frightens me. Seeing her in the now sinister sunlight
seems to fuse the fatal essences of love and death.

She glances at me as I sit down beside her,
and after a second lets her shoulder slowly slump against mine.
I'm delighted: it's the closest we've been in weeks. With my free hand
I transfer my hat from my head to hers. Instantly she stiffens.
This sun is hard on the skin I say. *You should keep yourself covered.*
Please don't give me orders she says quietly. *It drives me crazy.*
Surprised, I say *Oh— I didn't mean to; I meant it for your good.*
Yes, she says *but it's always what you mean, or you believe, or think—*
which is always a veiled, or even open criticism of me.
It's humiliating she goes on *—it makes me very angry.*
Oh God, I think *another childish way of asserting herself.*
Don't you ever feel? she says, breaking the silence.
I start to be irritably amused by that
but then resolve to leave emotion to her, because it hurts less
to keep mine concealed. *Sometimes* I say. And add: *One becomes resigned.*
Never! she says, turning and looking straight at me. Seconds go by.

At last I say *Okay, our world has changed. It's become uncertain.*
And a bit scary. I don't want anything to happen to you.
Oh, ketzel . . . she says, using the Yiddish for kitten. And she smiles.
It might be a smile of triumph — I don't care: it's also loving.
Taking my arm, she says *Well, whatever comes, we'll cope together.*
I start to think *That's so naive—!* when suddenly it all makes sense —
she, I, our valley, our life here — all linked by the need to survive.
We'll try I say, feeling bared, but a lot better.

All my life I've loved women,
ever since I first sensed that they were somehow different.
Even as a child I was moved by the tender essence of them,
and later I admired the inner grace and strength with which they lead
their double lives, and I'm still always awed by the silent terror
inherent in their maternity. Ages haven't mattered:
I can be equally charmed by an eight or an eighty year old,
and at bottom it's only shyness, ordinary decency,
and social decorum — plus, of course, the risk of being got wrong —
that keeps me from embracing almost every woman I meet.
But up close, minute to minute, I no more understand women
than I do my wife; nor, and perhaps even less so, do I men.
No, what really goes on in any human being is for me
as much a mystery as the other enigmas of nature.

My darling is a product of the postwar age,
and wants to scrap anything that won't immediately work.
"I'll fix it" peeves her: she feels it's my personal, perverse whim.
Oh, forget it! she'll say. *I'll pick up a new one.*
She simply likes to spend and use freely, prodigally —
facial tissues fly in our house like flakes in a paper storm.
Hey— Esther, please try to think of the trees I say.
She'll toss me an impatient look and fling the crumpled ball
with the bored aplomb of a practiced player, while muttering:
Rigid, repressed— and, Jesus, a martyr complex . . .
Then she'll speed off to town to buy spice or nuts for a cake,
never thinking or caring that the driving triples the price.
So I'm not perfect she shrugs. *Well, go on, shoot me.*

The darker side of that dig — meant as a joke
but with a trace of rancor — is that soon after she came here
I shot a dog, a newish one. It was a favorite of hers, a big
handsome beast, almost two years old, and though well trained
to basic commands he had an unrestrainable streak
of wildness, a fierce will to do, at times, just what he wanted.

There had been many alarming incidents.
He had killed chickens and geese, and badly mangled a goat kid,
and often, bristling and with bared fangs, he had leapt at strangers.
But Esther petted and cuddled him, and took him for walks,
and believed that she alone had a real rapport with him.
Then one day, in front of her, while she, horrified, screamed *No, no—!*
he killed a cat. I said *It could have been a child;*
we can't take the chance. Shaken, she said *Then give him away.*
I said *That would only hand others our dirty work.*

    I led him; she silently went along awhile.
And then she said: *I love this dog. Why does he have to die?*
I knew what death evoked in her. I said *Well, what should I do?*
She looked down, shook her head, then quickly walked away.
The dog knew what was coming: that was much the worst of it;
he trembled as I held him and put a bullet in his head.
Now long ago. But that shot reverberates yet.

    My whole being caves in at the thought
of anything happening to her. When she goes out
I tremble and tell myself I might never see her again.
When she rides I dread her being thrown, and when she drives,
carelessly, as I always think, I try to pit all my will
against an accident. I know I can't seduce fate,

but the idea that all we have could suddenly be gone
reduces me to crushed begging — I don't know of whom.
When she returns, and before our conflicts can come crowding in,
it's like sunlight flooding the room, and when she at once comes
to my arms, as she always does, giving and wanting a kiss,
it's worth everything.

She's off again. Off to the city to see someone.
This woman phoned and said she needed help. Esther cried *Of course!*
And said to me *I have to go.* I nodded, thinking:
My love is lucky to be able to run off when she likes,
knowing there's nothing here that really needs her staying.
She's as much a steadfast farm wife as a swallow is a snail.
   Lilly, the woman who called, is, or was, living with
a former lover of Esther's, and we met her, and I him,
when he insisted Esther visit them, but I had
no idea then of what he'd been, and only wondered
why my wife seemed so wary of my going with her.
Later, when I asked, she soon readily admitted it,
but laughing, airily dismissed him as having been
of absolutely no importance. She said his one attempt
at lovemaking had been such a feeble, awkward fumbling
that they'd both been too embarrassed to go on.

He'd said she intimidated him, and she'd said *Well,*
then I always will, and they'd agreed to drop for good all that
was physical between them. And indeed, I'd noticed
his discomfort. And Lilly's! When we entered their apartment,
Esther — who goes mouth first into everything — cried:
Oh, you're moving! And Lilly, who'd so wanted to impress,
had to say *No, this is how we live.* Now there's this call for help.

Two days later, having heard nothing, I'm brushing
my teeth before going to bed when the dogs begin barking
and car lights sweep across the bridge. Then eager yelping
and Esther comes in. She looks listless, pale, tired. Her hair is loose.
I take her into my arms and she slumps against me,
but I can feel neither involvement nor relief in it.
What's the matter? I say. She sniffs, shrugs and backs away.
Are you okay? She nods, and undoes the buttons of her dress.
And Lilly? She pauses, drops her eyes, and raises them.
She'll be all right she says. Then: *That slimy bastard left her.*
He stripped the place while she was waiting at the doctor's.
Took even the money she'd been saving for the kid's layette.
She was pregnant? Esther barely nods; then tears begin.
What happened? I say, suddenly in dread of some assault.
She bled a bit. Otherwise she's just low, miserable.
And the baby? She's pulling off her dress. *How is her baby?*
Aborted she says. *What else was there? She has nothing!*
Troubled, I say *Welfare? A job? She's still got her looks—*
That's all she has— her ass. No other skills she says. *Can't even*
keep house. Could you see her on welfare? It would've been the kid who'd paid—

Christ, the world didn't need another unwanted child.
   I sigh, and a vague desire begins to vie with my distress.
I reach and touch her cheek with the back of my fingers,
and then her throat, and moving closer, tenderly cup a breast,
and then, palms held below, both, as if milk might flow.
She looks at me and I kiss her, her mouth warm but wondering.
If... I say, trying to word my feelings *I come from*
watching a sick person struggling to drink a little water,
I want a good meal. When I come from a funeral...
   Eyes bright, she says at once *I'll shower*— and starts for the bathroom,
but I halt her and hold on. *No,* I say *right now, please.*
Well, just let me wash— she says, but I'm pulling her to the bed.
Let's affirm life I say, stripping her and then myself,
and she, catching my fire, cries out when I, huge, go deep in her.
We thump, twist, roll in a noisy, mad, voluptuous,
volcanic frenzy, in which she, screaming, erupts endlessly —
until I too can't stop; and through final explosions
we sink slowly and then lie silent, spent, sweaty and smelly,
and feeling lustily alive.

   Helen, who seldom visits, has come again,
bringing a friend younger than Esther — a striking blonde
who's just finished her service with the Israeli paratroops.

Honey is her name, and her coloring: she must have some Yemenite
or other Arab influence in her genes. Her smile, though,
which crinkles her laugh lines, is altogether Jewish,
and there's a surprising softness beneath her strong bouncy stance:
when they came I met them first, and said *Welcome*
          and kissed her on the cheek,
and at once her look took on a loving glow.
      My Esther, naturally, soon noticed that,
and is busy ridiculing me in Honey's sight.
Along with an excessive lunch she's serving funny stories,
about the meager *after-forty* bread she's had to bake — because I
had asked her please to reduce her use of fats; and about
how *he never sleeps* — because I always drink a lot,
and sometimes wake up to pee, and then, most nights, will write awhile;
and how *he holds his horses* — because I don't, in most cases, it's true,
ride or act nearly as recklessly as she.
      I can't believe these knives dropping from her lips,
which slice me into someone old, frail, fretful, timid —
she's never been this flagrantly misleading or malicious.
And of course it's working: Honey looks from her to me with puzzled eyes,
not quite sure of what it is that's happening, but thinking,
I can see, that she'd be wise to keep well clear of it.
Esther always does this — an amiable discomfiting
that drives off anyone for whom I have some feeling. But, my God, why?
Why, of all women, should she be insecure?

Once, at a housewarming in the city, we met a woman
as superb as Esther, but with a much softer, more elegant air.
We sat talking with her on the porch while the party went on within.
Slowly opening her hand and spreading the fingers, she said:
Love must be like that . . . and looking at her,
      listening to her — who seemed
in thought, looks, poise, in every way related, like a work of art,
she seemed, for a suspended second, unquestionably right.
Then I began to wonder how her husband felt, and watching my wife,
who'd said nothing, I saw a hint of objection sneak into her smile.
If it's true, I thought — for we'd been speaking of desired lovers —
how does this lady manage it? Done secretly it's too demeaning,
and if openly, then much too painful for everyone involved.
I remembered the three fine women I had known at one time,
none of whom I'd misled, and how it was the missing moments,
my: *No, I'm sorry, I'm tied up tomorrow night,* and then her hushed: *Oh—*
which hurt most. It was those faint *ohs* that finally finished me.
I've never bed-hopped since. But now, would I go to this woman —
who insists that if loved she must be free to love — if she wanted me?
I'd be sorely tempted. Sitting here I can undress her, feel myself
enfolding her smooth thighs, sliding my hand from her flat belly
to her breasts . . . and finding her, as I'm sure I would, just as wonderful
in every other way — it's a teasing, euphoric fantasy.
But in reality there would be a lot to weigh and fear.

And what about her doting husband — though he seems to revel in her,
isn't he as free, and is she willing to be less than first with him?
If she is, that's for me a fairness too much removed from flesh.
  I feel that my wife, despite her former lovers, started fresh with me,
and I'm always incensed by the thought of any alien intrusion
into her, into what I now think of, fondly, as a shrine.
And mine: though I say, and know I don't, can't, personally own her,
I feel the mating act is mine, as if that tie were territory
from which all trespassers, all, must absolutely be kept out.
  Yet if I dare reproach her, I'm made to look and feel foolish,
as if my suspicions prove me irrational, small-minded, crass, vain.
Once when I mentioned the many times she'd been alone with the potter
she said *Well, I needed that. And you didn't choose to join us.*
And anyway, he didn't get into my pants. We preserved your pride.
I felt shorn of it, and said that I was flabbergasted she would think
it depended solely on that technicality. She shrugged;
I could have hit her. But now, seeing her chin nod
          while her mouth demurs,
I know well my pride of possession takes in her whole complex person,
and that I want her admired, feeling her glory sheds on me.
But I, who am plain, shy, no talker, and committed to fidelity,
who has no money, and whose worldly prospects aren't exactly bright —
indeed most men don't understand why she's with me — why does it
immediately matter if I'm warm towards another woman?
And really, more puzzling yet, is that it's perfectly apparent
that this double standard seems to her not only fair but right.

Thomas and Esther are having tea at our picnic table,
she sitting pertly on top and he at her feet on the bench below.
Thomas and I are dressed alike today, in green work shirts and trousers,
rubber boots, and caps — his the baseball, mine the small-peaked kind.
I'm off to chores, but Thomas has just come from the local abattoir,
where there's a government inspector in a clean white coat and helmet,
and farmers bring cattle, pigs, sheep, goats, and later get them back
as neatly-wrapped steaks, roasts, stewing meat, hamburger,
        suet, and sausages,
or smoked bacon and hams, and it's all done with a minimum of fuss:
a numbing rifle shot to the back of the frightened beast's head,
and then it's strung up and its throat is cut, and the gushing blood runs off
in an open drain in the concrete floor; then the carcass is gutted.
    Thomas had a Holstein cattlebeast killed a few days ago,
and he's brought us the parts he says his wife won't use:
        the liver, sweetbreads,
tongue, heart, kidneys, and oxtail, and a bag of bones for soup or the dogs,
who are hotly sniffing the rank, exciting smells on his boots.
    I'm not jealous of Thomas in the ordinary sense,
but I envy, while I admire, those qualities in him Esther loves:
that he can awe her — sometimes stop her heart —
        with his innate gentleness,
his utter lack of guile, his blissful, endearing innocence.
And that he makes her laugh! If I were to say or do the things he does

they would seem affected, unfunny, tasteless, insipid, or absurd.
I doubt if there's ever anything physical between them,
a hug perhaps, if that, but I can now understand why some spouses
would rather have their wife or husband be physically unfaithful
than have them be captured by another's character.
That caring sympathy, felt tenderness, and sense of intimacy
can, without any touching, maddeningly shut out the lawful mates;
nor, for the excluded, is there comfort in their mutual state.
Once, talking about how wonderfully Esther and Thomas got on,
I warmly put my arm around his wife's shoulder in fellow feeling,
and she, looking overly burdened, leapt away as if burnt.

That night when we're in bed I say to Esther:
You really love Thomas, don't you? She turns from the magazine
she's been reading under her small white spotlight
and squints at me. *It's not the same thing* she says.
Where you touch me, in any place, bubbles begin in my body,
and they bubble up and up until they overcome my brain.
She moves closer, her hair brushing my shoulder.
Nobody else does that she says. *Nobody else ever has.*
She says, as I touch her *It's your hands I love.*

We are happy, and woke to this happiness
without any special reason for it. At once the rest of the world
seemed far away, and everything around us just as it should be.
Esther opened her eyes and laughed, and I hugged
her wonderful body and kissed her breasts, and she joined me
      for breakfast,
which is rare, and we had hot waffles and yogurt with maple syrup
and homemade cappuccino, and it was all,
in both flavor and our doing it, delicious. Now we are languid,
not in a hurry even to make love. The sun is softly shining.
We seem to have all day, all our days, as if
our joined life will never end. This rare sense of body and mind at rest,
of being complete and content, is the best holiday we could have;
we are, for the moment, even without fear.

Now to every friend who phones Esther cries *Come out*—
and they do: we're continually busy with guests arriving
and departing, eating, swimming, sunbathing and so on, and the house,
shamelessly crowded, is never still. At all hours, except for near dawn,
when even the nightly sighs and snores seem somewhat hushed —

I like to breakfast and be out before the others rise — it's filled
with human sounds, and above all, like a singsong tumult, with talk.
    Talk is, of course, my wife's medium, the chief vehicle of her charm,
and these confederates are an added catalyst: Esther talks
while she cooks, and when she serves, and while we're all waiting
for her to sit — she'll go on and on until the collective hunger
causes me to shout *The soup's getting cold*— at which she becomes irate
and cries *Well, why aren't you eating!* and refuses
to continue, though our contrite expressions now all beg her to,
and then with a laugh that instantly clears the air she'll colorfully tell
the rest of it — her gossip, news, or comment. Meanwhile
        we're freed to eat.
    Her talk for company is a kind of performance,
but there are also long private periods when she mostly listens,
when people pour out their lives to her; she has that immediacy
that makes others feel she'll have insight and empathy they mustn't miss.
    Unless these stories are confidential, I hear them
in bed, where we whisper and try to gag our giggles, like about
Betty — whose house was burgled twice in one week —
        asking her new lover,
as she was going into a store to buy sweaters, whether he thought
the thief would like green or blue. But often they're quite sad,
these accounts, baring our visitors, exposing vulnerability.
Are you asleep? Esther says, after we've both drifted into silence,
and ignoring my *Not now* she says: *Betty was once badly abused.*
Sexually? I say, shocked into grief and rage. *When?*
When she was ten. Today's the first time since then she's talked of it.

My wife, tense, pauses, and then says *I don't want a rapist shot or hung.*
It's too fast. I want blood; I first want his balls ripped out, slowly . . . very.
    Although most of our guests offer to help with the work,
and some, unprompted, do set and clear the table, or wash dishes,
and all feel they have to go at least once to the garden or stable,
we usually regret it, because they make more work than they do.
This week Helen's divorced doctor friend pitchforked his foot,
and had to be taken to town for stitches, which lost half a day,
and now, glum, he lies irritably waiting for the end of their stay.
And Esther's French schoolmate phones Paris and Florence at our expense,
and Sheila's cousin, asked to weed the asparagus,
just wrecked the fronds that store food in the roots for the following year.
Did you tell her off? my wife accosts me with, adding: *I sent her back*
for corn, and she returns complaining that she's breaking more than she picks.
    I'll go I say. *That lady's a liability.*
That's all we have she says, laughing. *Grow extra, like for the raccoons.*
I grunt, but really I'm thrilled by my love's vivid, volatile largesse;
having our own human kaleidoscope dwarfs the cash drain, the distress.

    How calm it is; tranquil. No tourists.
September has spread a soft stillness.
We hear only sounds of the river,
the wind, sometimes rain, livestock, the dogs;

and each other when we care to speak.

All the garden is suddenly ripe.
In the evenings we can and freeze,
and are stacking up stuffed bags and jars.
It's easy now to be gentle, kind.
A good year, after all. We're content.

From a passerby who stops to talk
we learn that this morning Thomas was taken
to the county hospital. Alarmed, I phone there
and the operator searches for his room number.
Oh, here it is she says at last. Then:
Oh— The bored voice suddenly softens: *He's gone.*
Gone? I say, pushing away panic. *He's gone home?*
No, died. About an hour ago. Sorry, that's what's here.
I thank her, thinking: *Gone? Just like that?*

In the funeral hall we have only the idea of our friend;
we feel remote from the sunburnt farmers in their dark Sunday clothes,

and from their solemn-faced wives, and certainly from the wooden casket
resting on the bier. Thomas, if he were here, would surely say something
arch about it. His widow, though, looks stern; flanked by
       their two stalwart sons,
both high-steel workers, she's also supported by the code of conduct
this small community expects and understands. I remember that
when each boy dropped out of school, refusing to farm,
      Thomas calmly said:
Well, someone has to drive the trucks and build the buildings.
     It's hard to trust
what we've all been told, that his heart suddenly stopped in the hospital;
I half expect him to walk in now, slyly pretending, for a while,
that this isn't all a hoax. How we would laugh afterwards! However,
no one here shows any hint of humor; even Esther is downcast,
soberly dressed, hushed, but she privately presses her hip against mine.
   The sermon begins. The preacher informs us
      that Christ died for our sins,
and that He bodily rose from the dead and ascended to heaven,
and that He will return. *These truths,* he says *are beyond the slightest doubt.*
A few listeners nod, their response as routine as his well-worn words.
And all who are pure, he says *will join Lord Jesus in paradise.*
At this, just a trace of unease appears in the slightly frowning faces.
The preacher spreads his arms, as if gathering the flock. *But*— he cries,
pointing at the coffin *this man, who was taken by surprise,*
what was his state of sin? His voice rises to a scream. *There was no time*
for him to cleanse his soul! He went unblest, burdened by all his carnal,
catastrophic wickedness— the sort of thing any of you can slip into.

146

Take care. . . ! he shouts, warning his hearers to be prepared,
      but I am wildly
turning to those around me, looking for shared shock, for some denial
that this diatribe has anything to do with the Thomas we knew.
    However, their hooded eyes remain largely cast down,
      expressions blank,
backs somewhat bowed. Then I recognize it: the entire congregation
is like cattle huddled against a storm, suffering it, surviving.
But this too plunges me into deep depression. I cannot abide
that no one has said he was kind, that he lived an almost blameless life.
And even when it's over, outside, where people are pausing to talk,
I can't bring myself to join them, but work my way towards the widow,
who's stiffly waiting for the first car. Esther has meanwhile disappeared,
saying she'd be back in a few minutes. *We won't be at the burial*
I whisper, and Thomas's still pretty wife brusquely waves that aside.
I say: *He'll be greatly missed. By you, of course, most of all.* She looks up,
evenly. *Everything has its time* she says. *Kids one day leave home.*
It was like raising three of them. I've been very patient. Now at last
I'll have my own life. The car comes, she gets in. I'm left of all bereft.

    This time you won't have to celebrate life Esther says
when we are home. *I slipped away there to go to the drugstore,*
for the result of my test. She coolly meets my incredulous stare.

It's as I thought . . . she continues. *I'm rather pregnant.*
Pregnant! Bewildered, I say: *Are you sure? When did you suspect?*
Shloymeh Yoyneh shluft mit zien vieb . . . she begins, teasingly intoning
an old Yiddish saw about a comic everyman
who sleeps with his wife but doesn't know the color of her eyes.
I've missed my last two periods she says. *And you really haven't noticed?*
I shake my head, still totally stunned by this surprise.
It happened after I told you about Lilly— Esther laughs.
That was some affirmation! And suddenly I clearly recall
our ardent lovemaking. *I would have put something in,*
she says *I knew I was ovulating. But you wouldn't wait.*
She comes to me, where I've sunk down on the sofa, and sits on my lap.
I feel I'm holding two fragile living creatures.
Her fingers stroke my neck, push into my hair: *Well, it was time.*
It's news that we were scheduled. Yet I sigh and say: *Yes. I'm overjoyed.*
You are? she says, seriously scanning my face. *Really?*
Esther— I say, gently moving her aside and getting up,
because I need some space between us *what makes you think I wouldn't be?*
It matters she says. *A lot.* I see her so intense,
seized on me, and it's irritating. *Why is this an issue?*
I say. *Hell, it could have happened anytime— with all your lovers.*
I ran from them! she cries, surprising me with her heat.
Oh, I reply *I think you often stumbled along the way.*
You don't understand she says fiercely. *I didn't unpack. Never once.*
Until you. I unpacked only when I came to you.
   In you, she says *I sensed what I want for my children.*
That's why I came back each time I went away, that's why I've stuck it out.

148

And that's why I'm here to stay. She stops, her face flushing.

    I'm deeply flattered, but I feel that this flattery
is subtly, steadily, with threads like silken steel, binding me,
and that everything about that passionate girl sitting there
is terribly strong, and that I'll be totally trapped
between her beauty and her new, pressing need of protection.
But I say: *I've got some dry birch in the workshop. I'll make a cradle.*
What matters, she says *is whether you'll love my— our, child.*
How can I not? I say, a little annoyed now. *I love you.*
No, she says *you don't. You did love me a little for the first few days,*
and since then I've sometimes seduced you, made you jealous,
or anxious, and occasionally I've driven you crazy,
but that isn't love. You've always managed to stay just your side of love.

    I feel the force of this, and suddenly see myself
as still alone, with my loneliness cushioned by this lovely
vital creature who shares my bed, my house, and most of my outer life.
I remind myself that I'm the luckiest of men,
that she came just in time to save me from solitary madness,
and that she's given me a feast of sensuality, and new friends,
and an almost constant kind of mental excitement,
and that there's no other woman in the world I'd rather have.
And yet — oh God — whatever it is that truly makes two people one,
if it exists, I've failed to find, or to fulfill it.

    Well, I say sincerely *I appreciate your faith in me.*
I feel safe with you she says. *I feel whatever comes, even the worst,*
you can be counted on. I want that for my children.
She smiles: *Though it hurts that you don't love me, I can live with that;*

love comes and goes, and yours might come again, and anyway I love you.
This time that's startling. *And badly as you think of me,*
she goes on *darling, this child we're going to have is guiltless . . .*
I don't want it unloved. I want this baby to have every chance.
I can't answer her. My feelings are too confused.

3

THE
LONELINESS
WITHIN

We're alone. The professor has left for Rome,
much amused about getting a research grant
for taking the same trip any tourist might.

I'm glad he's gone. He's bright, and we both like him,
but his presence sometimes spoils our privacy,
our sense of having the valley to ourselves.

The night's been cool here; my bride, half asleep,
shifts closer, and curled, huddles against my side,
needful, sheltering her nearly vibrant child.

I should get up. But I linger in our warmth,
letting my midnight thoughts take on waking shape,
and watching the moody, windswept sky grow light.

Well, it's taken me months to see that all is changed.
My rash wife, who was always ready to run off
at the least hurt, or any random unmeant slight,

is taking root and preparing her needed nest,
reducing stress and doing what is easiest,
and seems to have her life all tidily arranged.
 While I, who wanted only that she shouldn't leave,
now feel stuck with her, or at least with this warped state,
in which all we have and are inclines to her,
like our entire watershed draining to the sea,
and nothing of real importance depends on me.
And it's something about which I can hardly grieve.

 Whether I'm compensating for my lack of purpose,
or using up idle drive as outdoor work declines,
whatever it is she's never seemed more delicious,
and my desire holds, increases, even while indulged.
Her whole body's rosy with an inner joy and strength;
her skin seems, incredibly, even smoother for it,
her shining hair falls in flowing waves to her shoulders,
and all her forms are full in the most inviting way.
She's like a good-humored goddess who's available,
and doesn't care, so long as it's loving, what she does;
while she's nude I relish, drink in, all I can of her,
and when she's dressed, well, I try to see her as she was.

Without waking her I slide out and softly light a fire
in the Franklin. Its sudden, welcome heat soon reaches her
and she stirs, sighs, calls out *Good morning, my man . . .* and smiling
comes to me, quickly covering her bareness with a robe
that doesn't quite close on her bosom, so I have her breasts
for our snuggling embrace, but she soon breaks away, gasping:
Got to pee!—and makes for the bathroom, laughing back at me.
Just watching her go I'm becoming warm, as she well knows,
so when she comes out, amused, with her face washed and teeth brushed,
she lets me lead her and lie her down on the braided rug
beside the purring stove, and when I smugly spread her robe
she says pertly *Where's the night gone? It seems we've never stopped.*

She's been to some high-powered doctor she met at a party,
whom apparently she so charmed that his pained wife left in haste,
along with my beloved's date — that was before she'd met me,
and I imagine that her first appointment with the doctor
was more than purely professional; but we can't do better,
because he's both a professor and now the hospital head
of obstetrics, and is, I've heard, nice, and has obvious taste.

His blunt opinion was that she's in perfect shape, has good health,
and should have no trouble at all; or rather, not with him.
When she asked him, anxiously, about lovemaking, he just laughed
and said *As you like— if it pleasures you it'll probably please
the baby too.* So she's reassured about all the basics.

We're in bed, making repeated, magical love,
in which every touch, move, response, is . . . yes, truly ideal;
our mood, the fire-warmed air, and the pure soft moonlight streaming in,
reflecting from the tall wall mirror, are all just right for it.
Mmm . . . she murmurs, recovering. *We should do this more often.*
You mean get you pregnant I whisper. *No more devices, eh?*
Oh darling, she says sighing *it's marvellous. For the first time
I feel totally free and completely nothing-but-me clean—
no pills, no diaphragm, no worry at the back of my mind . . .*
And no more doing it dry she adds, giggling. *That must have been
uncomfortable for you. Not a bit,* I say *it was fine.*
And so were all the generous, divine things you did for me.
For we had always managed, exuberantly, even when
she was stopped up during the strongest part of her periods.
But, I say, starting *nothing's like being fully inside you.*
For me neither she says. Then suddenly: *Darling, do you think
God is jealous? No,* I say *She-He do this too, all the time.*

156

It's what keeps the world going. Yes . . . as she tightens *sex-sex-sex—*
life's luscious sweetening. She shudders softly. *But, as you said . . .*
her voice already thick with sleep, she trails off: *they both know that.*
I kiss her gently, and keeping her close, slowly settle down.
Merde . . . she says then. She knows the word a dozen different ways.
What is it? I say. *I just thought* she says *of all the women,*
men too, who don't have this. What gets them through life? Lord we're lucky.
Yes I say, as she sighs and sleeps again. I lie beside her,
faintly seeing her face and shoulder, and her beautiful breasts,
and I think: *Yes. But then, why don't I love her best?*

Because these nights my mind is full of memories
of all the wonderful women I have known, or so they seem
in retrospect, now that the irritations of those amours
are past. I no longer yearn for ties; granted, I have all that,
and yet . . . oh, sometimes remembered moments with other bedmates
offer more charms than the coupling actually taking place,
and the made-up hills, vales, and nectar of another body
are more satisfying than the real one writhing in my arms.
Yes, I assume it's the prospect of the baby that brings on
these spectres, but why? It isn't as if we'd ever agreed
to have no kids, or that I don't want them; on the contrary,
I find the idea of being a father flattering,

and even have buoyant images of a big family.
No, it's . . . it's something deeper that disturbs my mind.

The day's been cool and gloomy, with a brisk flurry;
I've brought to the kitchen what was left in the garden,
and Esther is washing beets and carrots at the sink.
She's showing now, and wearing an old shirt of mine
with the front panels pushed apart by her belly,
and underneath, blue jeans — a man's pair, partly unzipped
and held by braces that straddle her bra. She's barefoot
of course, and her long, loose, curling hair
        hangs like an unstrung floor mop.
Just as I've loved the few times I've seen her totally elegant,
I hate this sight, and say *You look like hell. Jesus, why can't you wear*
a decent dress— a maternity one, I mean. She squints at me
resentfully and says *I will. Miriam is lending me some.*
I'm about to say *Oh, come on, we could afford a new one—*
but then I can't be sure: we're depending on our rye-crop payment,
and even when it comes, what with deductions for foreign matter,
and maybe moisture, we might do no better than cover costs;
all our cash goes to pay the mortgage, taxes, other such musts.
But I remark, impatiently *It wouldn't hurt to brush your hair.*
And she pales and says *It's still wet.* What's particularly baffling

about this disregard is that her tattered clothes are always clean,
and her body ever fresh and subtly fragrant; I used to think
that was the natural scent of her skin, but I know now
it comes from the sparing use of an expensive perfume
she picked up in France when keeping a tryst with the man who died,
who inconveniently had a wife. The thing is, why won't she
visibly enhance herself? — though it's true that despite the disarray,
behind it, revealed at every turn, there's a lovely face and form,
and now that she's slightly arching her back, to balance
        the weight in front,
she moves with more grace than ever. But she doesn't do all this to tease,
I'm sure of that; there's a barbed, almost armored air about it.
Mark me down— she says dryly, but with a bite. I stop staring
and decide to let it go, at least till dinner.

When we're finishing our coffee,
and comfortable, and she's a little more flexible,
I say softly *Darling, why do you dress so badly?*
She says *Because I haven't any clothes. You do,* I say *some,
and that closet full of castoffs.* Then, more mockingly than meant,
I add: *You know, skirts can be let out, tops adjusted,
I presume that's what most preggies do. Ket-zel . . .* she says
do I disappoint you? You should have another wife for show.

No! I say. *One's quite enough. And I don't want anyone else.*
But tell me, is this it? Was it always? Didn't you ever care
to dress well? What about for all those rich men you could have married?
She shakes her head, smiling, then says *It used to drive my mother mad.*
She'd look at me and then at God, wring her hands and sigh, and getting
no answer high or low would wind up hurling her worst curse:
— now I'm smiling too; for I know the sting of those sayings —
"May your children do to you" Esther recites *"what you are doing to me!"*
We both laugh, and that lightens our mood considerably. And she goes on,
evocatively: *As a kid, I soon learned it was safer.*
I . . . felt that if I didn't look nice no one would notice me.
You mean pigs I say. She nods. *Especially the pawing kind.*
But girls too. I really didn't want them to resent me more.
Shamed, I feel remorse mingled with admiration, and see her
isolated by her beauty, her irreverent humor,
the irresistible charm of her high spirits. *So all your life,*
I say *you've been essentially alone. And running* she replies.
It's only here I've stopped, with you.

I'm always moved by her, and that distracts me,
but when the ferment of my thoughts and feelings
has had time to settle, then I still come back
to the same nagging need, the need, for my sake,

to have her flawless. She's my bright shield, my thrust
against all that's ugly, dull, and ominous,
and, too, against the touch of time. More, it feeds
my grown pride to look at her and think she's mine,
and to garner the prestige of her appeal.
But basically what bothers me is that
she's become integral to how I relate,
both in and outwardly; she's infused my mind
and soul, become an innate, real part of me.
What would now be left if she should cease to be?

My deep fear is that she might die in childbirth.
It's purely irrational; there's no reason for it,
except the subconscious hope that it will happen.
Then at once I'd be rid of her, and perhaps the child,
and all the complications of competing with them.
I'd revert to the easy task of just existing,
of getting through each day with a satisfied stomach
and not too much boredom, or, more profoundly, panic;
I can see the attraction of armies, religions,
terrorism, born-againism, and creeds of every kind —
certainty is much simpler than facing the puzzling,
frightening complexities of the problems for which

there are no solutions, of questions without answers,
or, as with me — of dangers that bar my defenses.

The clean new cradle is already in our room.
I made it carefully, copying from an old catalog,
but, lacking a lathe, instead of round spindles for the basket
I made the sides of smooth upright slats mortised into the rails,
and the ends, like the bottom, solid, but with a slight outward splay,
and held by two eyebolts hanging from hooks in the standing frame,
so the basket can be rocked, or removed and used on the floor;
and from firm foam rubber I cut a mattress and four bumpers
to fit close, and stitched tight white vinyl covers with cotton ties.
Esther, though she now cooks and cleans, still doesn't sew.
Work on the cradle kept me in the shop for hours,
and my wife grew wary of that, often wondering aloud
why I was at *that thing* so soon when it wouldn't be wanted
for many months, but now it's done she's pleased, and keeps it covered
with a woolen poncho someone gave her, which she never wears.
Oh, I know it was just what she didn't want, my dealing with
the baby in terms of metal and wood, but, allowing that,
it gave me an easily attainable goal, and time out
from the underlying turmoil that otherwise never goes.
I feel caught in a current stronger than my own.

No more wine my wife says suddenly, meaning our making it.
Why? I say, surprised. The winemaking has become part of life;
I've made hundreds of bottles, enough not only for our needs
but to take as gifts wherever we go, and to give away
to everyone who comes here. *It takes too much time* she says.
That's true; all our work sterilizing and washing, without which
we'd soon have vinegar, does involve a great amount of time.
Her implication is that we now have better things to do.
Perhaps. But I point out that there are still two full carboys clearing.
Good. That's great she says. *With what we've got, and me cutting way down
during the coming months, that should last us for years. Well,* I say
I guess we've kept our bargain. And we have: within days of it
she'd smoked her last cigarette, and I've certainly supplied wine.
That's right, she says *we don't have to prove anything anymore.*

While in the city I stop at a flower show
and bring my wife some apricot roses. She's thrilled.
They're not as stately as ours, and they have no scent,
but their coppery petals contrast strikingly
with the outside snow. *Flowers are the sex organs*

of plants, I say *but okay for public display.*
Yes, and you she says *are a pedant and a prude.*
Me? I cry. *Well, maybe unconsciously, inside.*
And, she laughs, fondling me *let's just keep it there.*
Hey! I say. *What is this— equal rights or something?*
Don't back away she says. *It won't hurt. Come to me—*
So supper gets cold while we sate ourselves elsewhere.
I love lustful banter and voluptuous play;
for long moments the whole sullen world spins away.

Early this morning, at breakfast, I hear on the radio
talk of an exact test for telling the sex of an unborn child.
Intrigued, I think about it on my way to town, to get a part
for the pump, and later, when I've got the water going again,
and Esther is up, and has showered, and is preparing a pan
of yesterday's good lasagna she's going to give me for lunch,
I bend over and slide my hand between the halves of her robe
and onto her bare belly, and she, smiling, snuggles up to me,
spoon fashion, and I tease her ear and hopefully mention the test.
Oh that— she says, straightening. *They draw off amniotic fluid.*
Well, I say *what do you think? Is it something you'd want to have done?*
Don't need to— she says with some scorn. *I know what we have. It's a boy.*
Pardon me, my seer! I say. *But would you please consult your stars*

and also tell me the next race winner, and when the world will end?
Schmuckie— she retorts *if you were at all educated, you'd know*
the Torah says if a woman spills her seed first it'll be a boy,
and you, my stallion, always have me spilling endlessly. She laughs —
If I had any business sense I'd put you out for stud.

Miriam has arrived with the maternity dresses,
and she and Esther talk nonstop about pregnancy, birthing,
babies and child rearing, and though they breathlessly disagree —
brisk Miriam, whose kids came bang-bang-bang, cries *Etti, that's bullshit—*
you've got to get on with life— natural birth and breast feeding
are nonsense!— while Esther, ardently inexperienced, cries *No!*
They're crucial— all caring communicates! — Miriam's charged presence,
always concrete and compelling, raises another small wall
around my wife's already self-absorbed circle of concern,
leaving me, the mere spiller of sperm, outside, and mute again.
Not that I'd add much; against those two goddesses, who give life,
my thoughts scarcely count. Besides, I'm with Esther. I was first drawn
to one fine woman, long before she and I became lovers,
because I saw her nursing her child, and was much moved.

Esther has seen a calf and a colt born,
and sometimes goat kids, when I've had to help a heaving doe
who was having two or three, and she's bottle-fed a few
their mothers abandoned, as goats often do when they have
more than two, or feel there isn't enough milk for them all.
So my wife's quite familiar with the natural process
and doesn't see why it should be much different for her.
Nor does her doctor discourage that; he's all for home births,
and thinks she can have hers right here, in the culpable bed,
with, if need be, only me standing by. But he insists
we take prenatal classes; so now, suppressing all doubt,
we drive once a week through twenty below and blowing snow
to stand in a class with other keen, embarrassed couples
and learn to breathe in and out, in and out.

The doctor is nominally in charge of all this,
and he did lecture once, and Esther introduced us,
and I found him handsome, and here-and-now, and, yes, nice,
but it's a nurse who conducts the actual classes,

and she's a knockout, with big dark eyes in a nun's face
and sleek, silvery-blonde hair that curls in at her throat
and a figure she manages quite subtly to flaunt
beneath the nicely-filled, crisp white, professional coat.
All that pale allure and sensuous, aloof appeal
calls to mind nothing so much as a Siamese cat;
and when she moves among us, demonstrating, faulting,
giving me help, I take in far more than her teaching.
In each class, she informs me, she has her favorite:
in ours it's Esther, and I've been included in that.

When she's not with a class or hurrying through the halls,
Nina — short for Janina; her people were Polish —
works with other nurses in the Prenatal Clinic,
where there's a small room in which she interviews patients,
asking about their attitudes, and then programming
the answers on long pink forms. Esther left her purse there
and when I go back for it, Nina is now alone,
with the purse on her desk. She hands it to me, saying:
Too late— I emptied it. Well you're quite welcome I say,
and we smile at each other in a promising way.
Where's your wife? she says. I reply *Peeing, down below.*

She pokes me playfully, but then the doctor comes in,
and at once her entire arsenal is turned on him.
So that's it! I think. *I should have guessed it long ago.*

But Esther says no, she has the hots, but not for him.
I feel a competitive urge, and ask: *Then for whom—*
certainly not me. She dropped me like I'd disappeared!
Sure, Esther laughs *the most you are is a scratching post*
for touching up her claws. You, schnook, can't do zilch for her.
I don't get it I say. *What's she want? Look,* Esther says
the dear lady's divorced, desperate and determined.
He's both her boss and her advisor on the thesis
she's doing based on that dumb statistical study.
She's close to forty and feels her life's been a failure,
but still means to make her mark, so— she'll use all she's got.
I say *Were you told this?* She shakes her head. *Well— I thought*
you didn't know women. I don't, she says *but that much*
was obvious. Yes, maybe, I think *but not to me.*

After that, Esther and I are rather tentative
all week. That brash tongue of hers, I know, often hides hurt,
and though she still gives herself as gladly as before,
it seems slightly less spontaneous, as if within
she's drawn back a little from her skin. Which I deplore.
Not that I've done anything wrong — she'd even be first
to say that, but that I might have been open to it
causes her, I feel, a sapping sense of being frail,
and veiled tremors of abandonment and betrayal.
It wasn't meant to be like this, of course. Both of us
were supposed to be free *short of any carnal act*,
but the fact is, she's now specially vulnerable.
So I say no more about Nina, yet think of her;
for she's become the focus of all my fantasies.

These days I lead a dual existence,
coping with my current vague dissension
while dealing with the daily outward chores.
Because my wife is now preoccupied,
I alone muck out the stables, bed down

and feed all the animals, milk the goats —
trudge back with the milk through the deep fresh snow.
Then out on the tractor to clear the roads;
and when I've done that for almost two hours,
it takes as long to warm me up again.

Indeed, since mid-December we've been in the cruel grip
of crushing cold, without letup at all in January,
or in the first half of February, until finally,
a month late, the temperatures climbed to just below freezing —
for two days. And that was it: that was the thaw! And now we're back
to frigid sub-zero lows. *Jesus, what a winter,* I think
to be driving to classes. And still we go, sometimes leaving
an hour earlier if the weather's getting worse. For Esther,
having a natural birth has become something sacrosanct,
a holy, exalted act, demanding devoted study
and sober preparation; she's already put together
a kit of oils and spices, and plans to get a suction pump,
which I'm supposed to learn to use. Classes are like weekly church,
with even its social side: before going home most of us
meet for coffee and muffins, and kick around gossip and news.
But there's no talk of Nina, not about her personal life;

only my wife seems to have come to such a damning judgment.
I wonder if she did it for spite. Now that she can't, really,
she tells me the only reason she wouldn't soon go to bed
with another man is that I'd make such a big deal of it.

A few days later we're lying in bed after lovemaking,
and she wakens from some minutes of sleep and murmurs *Darling...*
I say *Yes*— And she says *I wouldn't actually do that...*
What? Go to bed with anyone else. Then I'm relieved I say.
And yet, there was a time, she goes on *one of those times I left,*
when I was very tempted... Where? I say. *Christ! In the city*
she cries impatiently. *But do you know what kept me from it?*
He botched I suggest. *Anything but* she says. *What held me back*
was the thought of all I'd lose. You mean in me? I say, smiling.
She replies *It wasn't property...* I lightly kiss her lips,
wryly thinking the lesson I'm meant to learn from this small tale
is uncommonly crystal clear; the hint of hanky-panky
with Nina must be bothering her more than I knew. I say:
Don't worry— neither am I likely to give up all we've got.
I hope not... she says, seeming to slide silently into sleep.
I can't. I'm troubled by her being that needy, and fragile.
I don't want Nina — I was only intrigued by the allure.

And yet I don't feel right, don't feel part of what's happening here;
even when inside my wife, with that big belly between us,
it's not as we were. Lying beside her, I feel quite alone.

No, it's not the belly, that's okay; oh, I do have to be
a bit inventive, but it hasn't really impeded us
in any way. No, it's . . . this terrible loneliness I feel,
an inner emptiness nothing can fill, and yet that can twist
and knot into bitter pain. I can't contain — can't feel in touch
for more than minutes with even a single other being,
not my wife, not any of the remembered women, no one;
my memories — those I've developed into fancies, fade,
even the false sense of oneness that briefly comes from being
inside Esther, it too soon goes, leaving me solitary,
as before. I've all that's needed for happiness, and nothing.
Lying beside my love, beside her beautiful warm body
brimming with life, I suddenly want to weep from loneliness.
It's the baby — that small alien person growing between us —
who's brought this on, or rather my present consciousness of it;
certainly the baby isn't to blame — right now, all at once,
I love that little creature fiercely, like I love my own flesh,
but I know I won't be able to hold him, or her, either.

I feel, without shame, so sorry for myself, and for my wife,
and for all the futility of my unconnected life.

    As yet, the baby might have no reality for me,
but in theory I was well prepared for it — ever
saying that marriage was a mechanism for raising kids.
Indeed, it was I who proposed that because we'd both been
intimately involved with others, before marrying
we should be tested for all transmittable diseases.
We went to a plain-speaking pathologist who'd spent years
in a slum practice in which he was seldom paid, and now
that he's successful and renowned, still sees in his small home
a few unfortunates and friends like us; and he still makes
house calls, many of them, on old people whose sight of him
is stronger medicine than his prescriptions can provide.
He took blood samples, and soon let us know that if marry
we must, he could offer nothing medical against it.

The baby has begun to kick.
For me, that is; for its mother
it's been moving about for months.
Now I too can see the ripple
and feel it ride across her skin.
In spite of Esther's confidence
I'm still neutral about its sex,
wanting only a healthy child.

Bringing nursing things she's knitted, Sheila comes by bus,
braving the winter roads, and though the blacktop is dry
when I meet her in town, some snow blows on our way back,
making her so jittery: *Jesus— those wild whiteouts—!*
it takes strong hot tea and three stiff brandies to restore
her boisterous joy. Helen's sent a set of rattles,
and Betty a beautiful Moravian blanket,
but Esther's mother so far refrains, saying darkly:
Ladies, you do as you like— I don't tempt the devil.
Sheila, neophyte knitter, still muddles her stitches,
or talks so much she makes too many, and often ends

with warty clumps she claims are her own design. All day
there's the click of needles and the clatter of voices,
and laughter — happy laughter that echoes through the house.

One night when I pass Sheila's door — she's left it open
for heat from the fire — I see her duvet's half slipped off,
and softly step in to cover her. She turns to me,
her big breasts rolling under her gown, and then I think:
If I slid in— she'd probably be too surprised to speak—
and in a few seconds she could well be pregnant too.
It takes so little to make a child . . . but how massive
is the aftermath. She sighs in sleep, and of course
I leave, and rejoin my wife, entering her instead;
but for a moment she's Sheila, and then suddenly,
Nina. I feel highly guilty, though these transgressions
are all in my head. I reflect that though I'm already
a father, I'm far from being fully a husband.
I wonder, in their hearts and minds, how many men are.

And as I lie awake I begin to realize
I've been indulging selfish feelings, which, if unchecked,
can lead to destructive, searing, frightening effects.
That looming loneliness, though it can be dragon-like,
and choke or madden me, isn't really a something,
but an absence of what gives me my sense of balance,
my feeling of belonging, of affecting others;
but it's also a reminder that everything
can go wrong: that bleak dismay I've fought off all my life.
But damn it, I won't be dragged down like this, forced to crawl,
obliged to lie, then always suspected, dogged by guilt;
I withstand all else — and won't surrender to myself.
No, I'm going to enjoy all the women I love,
but within strict, if necessary, quite stern limits.

Yet at breakfast we're merry; it's Sheila's last morning
and Esther is marking it with masses of pancakes,
maple syrup, eggs, corn bread, our own yogurt and goat's cheese
— more, of course, than three or four or three times four could eat;

she, I and the dogs will be finishing it for days —
and Sheila is laughing happily, her breasts bobbing
like big bubbles, now quite free of any threat from me.
That episode in the night, indeed my whole peeved mood
of the past weeks suddenly seems silly — but just then
I see myself reflected in Sheila's scornful eyes:
an older man, scruffy, poor, plain, rather humorless,
perhaps fairly dependable — at best a dull frame
for the full-blown portrait of her bright, fruitful friend;
in large part I'm tolerated for what I provide.

Every visit involves some household upheaval;
with Sheila gone there's the pots, dishes, towels and sheets,
and the vacuuming of her room, which I help with,
though I hate the machine, a shrill monster that exacts
much payment in stress for its swift, spectacular aid.
I suppose this is my mute way of making amends
for mental infidelity, but at the same time
I resent my guilt and Esther's indirect control,
the more that it seems needed and inevitable.
It's natural that her priorities should now shift,
that she should favor the fresh, the emerging life;

I'll have to lump it — to learn that, with her, from now on,
my self-serving wishes won't ever again come first.
Well, I accept all that, yet it cools my lust for her.

Not that her appeal has in any way diminished;
her mouth, skin, breasts, and that triangular bit of brush
are just as welcoming, but I've somehow grown weary
of lovemaking, of tongues, entwined limbs, squeezes and sweats.
I lie in bed beside her and want to turn my back,
and when I do, just slightly offending her I feel,
she disarms me by lightly running her fingertips
over my shoulder blades, spine, and the nape of my neck.
Comforted, I turn around again and embrace her;
we kiss, and my hands go routinely to her forms,
and then, oh, almost before I know it I'm pushing in,
pulled, lured onward by her joyous warmth and juiciness.
And we make a very pleasant interlude of it,
but I'm just as glad to separate and lie apart.

It's now almost a week since we've been close in bed,
and it's gone on much too long for more excuses.
So tonight she says archly *Still have a headache?*
and I smile, trying to think of some smart reply,
something between wit and not wanting to hurt her;
but, uninspired, say only *Just don't feel like it.*
O—kay she says, too chirpily, and settles down
to sleep, night-hugging her belly with hands and knees.
In the ensuing silence I turn more away.
Then, behind my back, she says softly *I love you,*
and I nod, feeling it really costs her nothing,
that it's the indulgence of a conquering queen
from whom taxes are temporarily withheld;
and, warily, I drift off dreaming of dungeons.

This morning, when I was checking the mare's chipped hoof,
she abruptly pulled it away, and me with it,
so that I slipped on a large slick of fresh urine
and fell heavily forward, hitting my knee hard
on the heel of a shovel that crashed under me.

As it was more humiliating than painful,
I first dismissed it, but later began to limp,
and at lunch Esther made me pull up my pant leg
and we saw how blue and swollen the knee now was.
To bed! she said. *And I'm putting on an ice pack.*

Afterwards, from my prone position, I see her
going into the guest room. *To rest* she explains.
What's wrong with here? I say. *Oh,* she says *I don't want
to disturb you. That's absurd* I say. *Why would you?*
Well, she says *you haven't seemed to like me lately.*
Whether or no, I retort, stung because it's true
that doesn't mean, you know, you can't share your own bed.
She hesitates. *It's your room too* I say. *Come on.*
She does, and stretches out beside me, glad, I see,
to let the bed take the whole weight of her body.

We lie for a long while without speaking. And then
she says *How are you? Healed* I say. *The ice helps.*
Keep it on she says. *And don't get up till supper.*
What'll I do all day? I say, turning to her.
She doesn't answer; her eyes are shut. Mine take in
her swollen breasts, and the big burgeoning hill
beyond them, and the hem of her loose dress drawn up
on her bare legs. Curious, I raise it further,
enough to reveal no panties. *Well, pardon me*
I say. *Can't be bothered,* she says *around the house.*

She hasn't opened her eyes, and the idea
of surprising her now begins to form in me:

a prank, mixed with a kind of mischievous desire
both to have her and assuage her feelings a bit.
She squints but says nothing when I push her legs up
and apart, and only sharply draws in her breath
when I moisten her with my mouth and then gently
but eagerly enter her. She erupts strongly
a good few times, then says *And what was that about?*
Oh, I don't know I say. *Guess I can't be idle.*

It's Esther's last, **last!** appointment at the Prenatal Clinic;
our baby is due in less than two weeks. The doctor's away
lecturing somewhere, but his sub, after some poking about,
has ordered another ultrasound. *See, look there, there's the head—*
says the smart technician, and I, who've been allowed to attend,
nod at the faint flickering shape she's taking pains to point out.
Oh, says Esther, from the trolley *the picture's upside down.*
No, laughs the white-coated lady *not at all. Your baby's breached.*
Esther goes blank; I feel it like an inner blow. But it shows,
because the technician says *It wasn't indicated before?*
Well, not to worry. Babies will often turn around again.
When we're back in the office, the sub, a senior resident,
says he wants more lab work. *Why?* says Esther. He looks at her chart,
not her. *Well, your blood pressure's up. We'd like to check some new things.*

In the car she begins to cry. Tenderly, I take her hand.
It can't matter that much I say. *So, a few complications . . .*
But I see that all she built up is now starting to crumble.
Her sobs shake her; then she bends away, abandoning herself
to weeping. Thick snow is falling. After a while the soft thunk
of the wipers is a metronome for her moans. I lowbeam
the headlights, looking for ruts to steer by. Eighty miles to go.
We didn't stay for class. After the clinic she just wanted
to leave. When we bumped into Nina, who asked what's the matter,
Esther wouldn't answer. I said *Later— I'll tell you later.*
Now I offer: *Darling, we can't be certain until you've talked
to the doctor.* Through tears her eyes flash as if that's insulting.
All right, I say *but we really don't know what it means. It might
still be okay. I want to hear what the doctor has to say.*

He phones the next day. Sounds hearty, but wants her back
    for more tests.
We try to be optimistic, and that night I hold her tight,
indicating that we're together, come what may. After lunch

the following day, more relaxed, we set out in bright sunshine
under a blue sky, with only some snow blowing here and there.
We're happy, at least outwardly, when we reach the hospital,
and the doctor greets Esther with a friendly big hug and kiss.
However, when the test results are ready he invites us
into his office and says he has to be blunt. *The facts are,*
the baby's still breached, Esther's blood pressure is high, and— and this
is what we double-checked— her sugar is up. My dear, he says
to her *you're what we call a gestational diabetic—*
you become diabetic under stress, as in pregnancy.
Given all this, you must stay here, and I'll schedule a section.

Esther is crumpled in a corner of the hospital bed,
her face a wrinkled mass of misery. She isn't crying,
but in her tear-stained eyes there's an armed wall against what we all
are doing to her. I sympathize, but also, I'm amazed:
my wonderful young wife, with her luscious figure, dash, and flair,
who'd so much beauty, joy and certainty she could lavishly
scatter it, looks, now, frightened — and, yes, actually ugly.
But suppressing that I say *Darling, what can I do for you?*
Take me home— she cries. *I hate all this!* Torn, I say *Well, uh . . . wait—*
and I step into the corridor and run down its long length

to the clinic. There's no one about — *Christ!* I think *they've all left—*
when I see in Nina's room her and the doctor at her desk.
I stop at the door, distraught, trying to still my hard breathing.
They both look up. The doctor, not unkindly, says *What is it?*

She wants— I gasp *not a Caesarean— a natural birth!*
Yes, I know the doctor pleads, unable to escape his plight
as the high priest of my wife's religion, in which each child
welling freely from the womb proclaims the mother's dignity
and promises to reform the world. Relentless, I persist:
She counted on it, so much. She's crushed! Really, is there no way?
Look— I've helped a weak cow, lots of goats, even a cat . . . Could I—?
No, no! cries Nina, but the doctor silences her and says:
If you want to take her home and attend her yourself, you might,
by some miracle, have a healthy baby. But now, knowing
what I do, I can't support, can't be responsible for that.
And I, who knew it was useless, basely, gratefully give in.
Then go to tell Esther she must stay, while, alas, burdened with
having to feed the animals . . . my sad sigh seems saccharine.

In the dark, driving home alone, I'm haunted by my last look
at her unlovely face, which, the dire truth is, I was eager
to escape from. Damn it, appearances are crucial to me —
my feelings are mercilessly influenced by what I see.
I'm a moral monster, always have been; for even at first —
though Esther was thrilling, heady — had she not looked marvelous
I wouldn't have married her. And will she now become a drab. . . ?
Suddenly I swerve to miss a fast car converging too close,
and go into a skid, spinning round almost in a circle —
and when, quite shaken, I'm under way again, I'm reminded
of the frailty of life and the vain fleetingness of surface.
Yet . . . I want what I want, and unhappily begrudge its lack.
My car beams are flung into fantastic shapes by swirling snow;
the wind is rising, blowing crazed blasts across the icy road.

At night, huddled under extra blankets,
missing my wife's warmth, I wake more than once
and still hear brittle snow being hurled
against the windowpanes. And I recall
Esther's dread of violent, roaring storms

— until now, one of the few things she was
outwardly afraid of — and hope she's snug
in the hospital, and in no hurry
to find physical outlets for her woes.
I know, too well, how headstrong she can be.

There's no dawn; a dim grayness grows somewhat lighter
as the driven day emerges vaguely from the storm.
In the turbulence, many trees are being bent
to the breaking point; and yes, I see two have toppled,
their trunks already buried in the waist-deep snow.
Both the power and the phone are out, which bothers me,
because I can't phone Esther, but she'll understand —
last night, half-hourly, the car radio reported
the blizzard was also hitting the area
that includes the hospital. Apart from the phone, though,
I'm hardly inconvenienced: I have candles, food;
I can cook at the fire and make my basic toilet
in the stable, among the uncomplaining beasts.
This whole disturbance should blow over by evening;
then comes a day of cleanup, and the next morning
I can drive down in good time for the scheduled section.
Meanwhile I linger in the house, letting things go,

reluctant to shovel paths while there's still drifting snow.
Oh, if it wasn't that my guilt would make me pay,
I could quietly enjoy this enforced holiday.

I step out of the stable after doing chores,
and in the growing dusk the glow of headlight beams
comes faintly from the road; they stop, blink, forge ahead,
and I know it's not a snowmobile but someone
bucking the drifts, and instantly I catch my breath,
while my insides cave: it can only be bad news.
I run to the garage and jump into my jeep,
and gunning the motor, roar out to meet the other
on the road. I buck from my end, and he from his
— he has, I can just make out, a jeep like mine —
and when we near each other I recognize him:
a dour farmer who's on a different phone line.
He hollers to me: *Emergency— your wife called.*
Her water's broke. Hurry up— the baby's coming!

My first reaction is to run back to the house,
quickly bathe, change my clothes, pack a bag, bring some wine —
but in the same swift, vain second I realize
the time that would take, and then, perhaps as penance,
decide to go at once: animals have been fed,
the jeep is gassed up — I did that last thing last night,
all else can wait, and I'm warm in my coveralls
and parka, large wool-lined mitts, peaked cap and thick boots;
as well, I'm already part way to the main road.
My friend — he's been instantly promoted, of course —
is backing up in his own tracks, and I follow
in the trail he's broken. At the forlorn highway
he moves aside and waves sadly as I turn south,
probably feeling it's futile — this mad mission.

Ahead, roughly a hundred miles to overcome:
an imperial dragon, but this time a sprawling,
palpable one I can grapple with, will to will.
With grim fear I mount, in four-wheel, more and more speed,
finding that though there's been wide drifting through big gaps

in the windbreak, often, between drifts, the snow depth
is less than in the valley. It's hardly blowing;
I churn drunkenly from the low nose of each drift
to the next, sometimes backing up to buck again,
and again, but then getting through, and going on.
Now I feel grand: fit, senses incredibly keen —
my headlights especially bright on the dark air
and white snow, and I feel a swift rush of wild fun
whenever I crash head on, sending up, like smoke,
an exploded cloud of flying snow — through which,
for seconds, nothing can be seen. It's just as well
no other fool is on the road. So far so good.

    I pass the highway work station, and the dark plows
are there, waiting for their sleeping drivers, of whom
I think warmly — as a talisman — and wish well
on their hard all-night's work, which will surely start soon.
Then the highway police station, from where furrows
lead me more easily to the intersection.
The small plaza there is partly lit, and someone
with a front-mounted blade on a half-ton pickup
is pushing back mounds of snow. And, engine idling,
with cab light on, there's a cruiser, a policeman.
He stares at me concerned, but only nods, because
at that point, where I've been slowing for the corner,
I'm not speeding. When he can no longer see me
I get out, hurriedly survey the scene, decide
what seems, at best, the least-risky route, and roar on.

More drifts, more bucking, but not stuck. Many miles more,
and there, swinging out from a second work station,
is a snowplow! I revel in the sudden ease.
   But the huge, blue-blinking brute moves slowly, pushing
so much snow, I'm trapped in the continuous trough
it's clearing. I can't pass it, and my swift delight
at tires on pavement soon curdles to anxious rage.
At last it turns into a dimly-lit truck stop,
and I, freed, fly ahead. And a little farther,
and from there on, the road is cleared. I've been moving
from the boondocks towards more built-up areas,
where plows have already been busy, and judging
from the height of the banks, the snow was less severe.
I'm truly afraid to look at the time; I feel,
with terror, that I'm well into a second hour,
with still almost half the way to go. And this is
civilization, with some traffic, and forced stops.
But between them I skim along, sliding sometimes
on icy stretches, and hurtling through red lights
when no one's near, wringing from the old machine
all the speed it will give. More than I knew it could.

When I rush into the hospital, it's strangely quiet.
The halls are empty — everyone seems on holiday.
No one questions me as I go up the elevator
and swiftly down the corridor: the bottoms of my boots
are soft. There's someone in Esther's room, sitting by the bed —
who looks round — it's Nina! — and there's my wife, with or without
her child, I don't yet know. *Oh,* Nina says *we decided
to wait for the doctor. He'll be here soon— in a few hours.
She should be all right until morning. Congrats, you made it.*
Alarmed anew, I can't much comprehend a victory.
I'll leave you alone Nina says. And then she's gone, though I
don't see her go. I kiss my wife. She looks wan, defeated,
but, if anything, somewhat less frightened. At that moment
it's suddenly good to feel her warm flesh, see her body.

What happened? I say hoarsely, my face close to hers.
I willed it she says. We speak in whispers, because
her roommate is cut off only by a curtain.
My contractions started Esther says. *I liked them.
They were like period cramps, which I now hardly have.*

Then, when they became regular, I realized
what they were, and I was so pleased. Oh boy, I thought,
I'll beat the system . . . say nothing to anyone
and simply have my baby here in bed. Some hours
passed that way— happy hours. And then my water broke.

She goes on: *It was such a warm gush— I got soaked,*
and when I rose and ran barefoot to the bathroom,
my roommate— she's marvelous— she's had five fine kids
and this is the first high-risk— then she guessed what was
going on. "Dear, what are you playing at?" she said.
Nothing I said. "You're dripping on the floor" she said.
Well, I'll sit on the toilet till it drains I said.
"No, Esther" she called. "You don't know what you're doing!"
You do! I said. You can help me. Just be quiet—
"No!" she said. "It's not a game— this is serious!"

I cried: Don't you betray me! and locked myself
in the bathroom. But she must have called them;
a minute later an army was hammering
at the door. They said "open or we'll break it down,"
and when they took me out it was to a dry bed.
"You're a damn brat!" one said. No, no I said. Listen,
we can keep it a secret: I'll have my baby
here in bed, and it'll save the hospital money.
Then when my husband comes, we'll both be waiting for him.
I press her hand. Two single tears slide down her cheeks.

I don't notice Nina till the end of the corridor,
where she's waiting. *What about you?* she says. *Where will you go?*
That hadn't occurred to me. I say *Maybe a motel. . . ?*
And food? she says. *Tonight's a bitch. Nothing's open.* I sigh.
Then come with me she says. *My place is close. I'll put you up.*
We go in her car; mine's off the driveway, on the side lawn,
where the security men tell her it can stay till dawn.
On the way I'm chilled, and discover I'm completely wet
with sweat, from the tension of my drive. We travel ten blocks
and pull up at a low apartment house. Her car handles
perfectly in the snow; it's sleek and efficient, like her.
When she unlocks her own apartment door and we step in
she says *Could you wait here—* and coming back, spreads newspapers.
Now strip your outer clothes she says. *I don't need the manure.*

I think I'm silent in stockinged feet, but she at once perceives
and pours me a shot of brown liquor, emptying the bottle.
It burns at first — it's neat brandy, but between coughs it begins
to feel good. The place is small, plain, and tidy: a sofa bed,

table and chairs, TV, stereo, brick-supported book shelves.
There's a separate bedroom, but beyond the open doorway
it's dark. Nina hands me a man's bathrobe. *It's okay,* she says
it was my husband's. Go and shower. You'll find a razor there,
one I sometimes use on my legs. Take a fresh blade, and towels.
I do as I'm told, feeling relief and pleasure at being
in her care. There's some sexual innuendo, of course,
but her manner's neither provocative nor self-excusing.
We're much closer in age than either of us is to Esther,
and simply comfortable together; so, just now, it seems.

When I come out, completely refreshed, Nina's stirring something
on the stove, and at the same time talking on the telephone.
Yes she says. *Well— so so. Mac seemed satisfied.* Her tone is brisk
but deferential. She listens, frowns, and says decisively:
Then I'll scrub. To me, when she's hung up, she says *I just phoned in.*
That was the doctor; his plane landed sooner than expected.
He's seen Esther and thinks she'll remain stable. I nod and say:
What was that about scrubbing? She says *The scheduled O.R. nurse*
lives out of town, and says she's snowed in. No sweat. I'll take her place.
I'm bewildered, trying in all this to cling to something sure.
We're on at seven Nina adds. Then: *Soup and salad—* she says,
filling and serving our bowls. *Smells good* I say. *Soup's canned,* she says

but will have to do. There's also bread, a candle, an opened
bottle of wine. Nina's sipping from her glass, and now fills mine.

Before eating, she changes to a gray dressing gown, and looks,
with her silvery-blonde hair and dark mauve eyes, softly stunning.
Under our robes we're both nude — I see the pressure of her breasts
when she bends forward — and that begs a certain intimacy.
Nina, I say *why do you do it? Do what?* she says laughing —
Keep house? Have you here? No, I say *I mean work the way you do.*
She stops, and her big eyes, locking on mine, grow even larger.
I hope to do some good she says. *Against all the ignorance,*
I hope in my own way to make a difference. But I must
have status— honors, degrees. Without them, I'm nothing. I say:
You're very beautiful. She shrugs. *What can it buy me? It bought*
a marriage I soon didn't want. I say *No children?* She says:
Oh yes— a daughter, who's my delight! She's at finishing school—
and she goes swiftly into the bedroom, switching on the light.

There's a flood of femininity — pinks and greens, frills, flowers;
it washes back from that surprising room. She brings a photo
of a pretty, teenaged girl. *That— keeps me poor* she says fondly.
When she's sat down, facing me, I say *Nina, are you lonely?*
Once more those large eyes fasten tight on mine. *All the time* she says,
and something in me melts and moves to her. *Oh, my dear,* I say
but you haven't given up on love? She says *There is no love.*
People love only themselves. She stands up. *Leave everything*
she says. *I'm going to brush my teeth. You can use the sofa—*
there are blankets in the pull-out box below— or sleep with me.
My eyes widen. *Nina,* I say *you're the stuff of dreams— really,*
you've long been in my mind. But right here— with my wife where she is. . . ?
She says *What has one thing to do with the other?* I'm startled,
and she says *As you like. But now it's bedtime. I need some rest.*

When I join her in bed she gladly turns to me; eagerly
I kiss her face, her neck, her fingers. The forms of that body
surpass all my fantasies. Her breasts are firm, while I'm as hard
as I have ever been. God, I feel I'm in a living dream

196

in which every sense is satisfied, from the return touch
of her tongue to the soft caress of the silken, perfumed sheets.
Though I'm holding her, and it's tender, and altogether sweet,
I can't quite bring myself to lubricate and penetrate her.
My limbs feel as if they're locked by bars — my image of Esther
in her high-risk bed. I wait, wait, then at last capitulate.
God, I'm sorry I say. She pauses, then turns away to sleep.
In a short while she's breathing evenly. *I love you, Nina,*
I think *you're truly good.* And then, shocked, self-hating, I can't stay.
I grope to my clothes, the hall, the cold. It's not yet two o'clock.

Wandering the dark snowy streets, overwhelmed by shame,
I blame myself for having failed them both — beloved wife,
worthy would-be lover. That I hadn't intended
any harm to either seems of no importance now,
nor does it seem unreasonable to exalt them
and debase myself; in my morbid, remorseful state
all elements loom large. But the night cold penetrates,
and by the time I approach the hospital I'm chilled,
and tired. Shivering, I move the jeep to a safe spot,
and then, going into the darkened empty lobby,
sit, submissive, on a padded bench, slowly warming.

I don't venture upstairs for fear of raising alarms;
I feel I should wait for first light, or some morning stir.
After a time I doze, fitfully, for ten minutes.

When I go to Esther's room, she's already gone;
a shrewd nurse finds me and leads me to the scrub-up.
There I take off everything, down to my briefs —
and, when no one's looking, even them, because they're
not fresh — and don a kind of green papery suit,
complete with slippers and cap. Lastly, a nurse ties
a broad white cotton mask across my nose and mouth.
The operating room is a restless masked ball,
with, below lights, Esther lying in the center.
Her eyes are shut, and I'm afraid she's gone under,
but when I take her hand — we alone are ungloved —
her lids open and she says *Is that you, darling?*

Yes, dear, I'm here I say. *You're no longer alone.*
She smiles into my eyes, which are all she can see

of me within my queer costume. I recognize
the doctor from the clustering around him, and
Mac is the anesthetist — he moves me away
a little, not from Esther, but his equipment.
He probes her: she can feel nothing from the waist down.
Enough says the doctor. *Okay, can we begin?*
More lights go on. A square cloth on Esther's belly
is folded back. The doctor takes a scalpel . . .

   And — above the white mask of the nurse beside him —
I see those big, dark, mauve, unmistakable eyes —
which fill me with terror. The doctor makes a long,
curved cut. Blood spurts. Nina swabs, hands him instruments.
I think *Only hours ago I held her, that warm*
sensual being, and now she holds such power
of revenge— Nina my love, I think *don't do it—.*
Do what you will to me, but please, don't hurt Esther!
My wife says faintly *Tell me . . . They're— they're folding back*
your belly I whisper. *There are layers of it.*

   And blood and blood and blood. Nina, another nurse
swab it frantically, clip on clamps. Then I feel
Esther's hand going limp, and see her lids flutter.
Wait— cries Mac. *She's dropping down!* And in a second
he has a clear plastic mask over Esther's face —
nose, mouth — with a kind of thin corrugated hose
leading to it. She breathes in, gasps, then grows stronger.
Oxygen he says, answering my grateful look.
And to the others: *Wait . . . Well— you can go ahead.*

Together the nurses pull the opening wide.
　　Then the doctor reaches in and uncurls something.
He follows with both hands, twists, lifts out a baby —
a nurse cuts the cord and hurries the child across
the room. *Hey*— doctor says to us *you have a son.*
There's an uncertain cry — then a healthy bellow.
The nurse, bringing the boy in a blanket to me,
puts him in my arms. *I want him— bare!* cries Esther,
tearing off her mask. I place him, his skin to hers,
on her chest, and she pushes him towards her breast.
And after a few brief fumbles, he fastens on.
　　Though still scared, I'm astonished at this fierce life force,
at his trying for nourishment from her nipple,
while she's being sewn up below. I take my gaze
off them and, trembling, seek Nina's, and she looks up
with her great cat's eyes and there's twinkling joy in them,
and I utterly melt, seeing, God!, that for her
what happened had truly nothing to do with this.
And thick tears of shame and gratitude blur my sight,
and I put my hands on my son and his mother,
and feel the selfsame warmth that flows through all our flesh.

Nina, lovely, you'll never be my lover;
nor will all the Ninas I might ever meet.
If I could I would be tender to them all:
so many women I'll feel that way about.
But I'm bound for life to this one lying here,
bound now by a living, underlying tie
much stronger than the rise and fall of feelings.
And yet mine, when I recall last night, are mixed.

Damn, though I would do the same again
— no, I'd not now let it go so far —
I resent my self-imposed restraint,
and perversely blame my wife for it.
May she too one day feel my desire,
disappointment, loss, rage — even now
she's mad about her pink plump boy,
who has, plainly, quite supplanted me.

And that makes me yearn cravenly.
My fingers want to stroke her skin,
to burrow between the baby
and her breasts, to — yes, make us moist.
She's beautiful now: flat-bellied,
she's recovered all her curves,
and those grim, forbidding stress lines
are gone, as if they'd never been.

Her face is radiant;
and as I look at it
I see that sunlit joy,
that passion, verve, wit,
bright mind, free, wild spirit
I first fell in love with.
And, unbidden, that love
comes stealing over me.

She looks up. *My two men* she says smugly.
You mean three I say. *Then four!* she shoots back,
having forgotten nothing. I whisper:
Are you going to make love to him too?
She shrugs, smiling, and I know I'm lost — left,
as always, a dimension behind her.

Lowering his mask, the doctor says *Lookin' good—*.
Esther shifts to show him more of the baby's face:
Isn't he beautiful? You both are the doctor says.
And I feel just great! she cries. He laughs: *That's because*
you can't yet feel the cut. In a little while, soon,
it'll be pretty sore. I'll be around to see you.
Now including me, he says *Congratulations.*
And to you, doctor; I say *thanks.* He nods, leaving;
most of the others have already left. *Let's talk*
Esther says, firmly taking my hand *—while I can.*
We'll make it, won't we? Of course! I say, carried by
the strong current — that fierce life force — coming from her.
We're a family— she says, and indeed, I do

begin to feel that — that our circles of concern,
though separate, overlap at the little one.
I love you I say, meaning it, with a whole heart;
at least for the moment. *Love comes and goes* she'd said
and yours might come again. How wise she was, and is.
Fellow creature, who chose me of all men, man beasts,
to mate with — and I her; and we've begun to grow . . .

Now a nurse tucks blankets round both mother and son;
they're wheeling them away. Rapt, I start to follow,
then stop — remembering I'm still in green, unapt
surgical garb — and, aching, watch them till they're gone.
Oh, world . . .

*This book is set in Garamond, a standard
typeface used by book designers and printers
for four centuries, and one of the finest old styles
ever cut. Some characteristics of Garamond
to note are the small spur on the "G," the open
bowl on the "P," the curving tail on the "R,"
and the short lower-case height and very
small counters of the "a" and "e."*

*The text stock is
55 lb. Windsor High-bulk Cream*